White Psychology

The New Emotional Science

Designed To Calm Your Anxious Mind

Frederick Donatone III

Publisher's Note

This publication is designed to provide information and educational services to the average reader. The author made efforts to ensure that the provided information is accurate, efficient, and reliable. Nevertheless, the author is NOT responsible for omission or errors in the information provided here. The author is also NOT liable for results in the use or misuse of the information provided therein.

All rights to this book are reserved. No permission is given for any part of this book to be reproduced, transmitted in any form or means; electronic or mechanical, stored in a retrieval system, photocopied, recorded, scanned, or otherwise. Any of these actions require the proper written permission of the publisher.

***

fd@frederiiick.com

TABLE OF CONTENTS

INTRODUCTION

Can't we stop the manipulation of people's minds?

The mind is the most delicate thing in the human body. It is the most sensitive and functional element in the human essence. If anything can be called your inner self, it is your mind. It is the thing deep down your body that commands your system. In case you have not noticed, your mind gives the power to every fiber of your body and soul. When your mind clings to something and wishes that you succeed in it, you will find the energy that you didn't know you have. And you will chase these goals in a way that you didn't think you could ever hunt a vision.

An awkward fact about the mind is that it cannot be touched or held — you cannot even tell where exactly your mind is in the brain. Yet, it is at the helm of whatever you feel or believe. As Muhammad, a famous religious leader says, "Whatever happens to the mind, happens to the body."

In your innermost thoughts, your strengths, failures, and feelings are decided. Whatever you feel there can sprinkle around and radiate all over your body. If you are happy in your heart, you will be satisfied down to your marrow and spine. If you have a weird, awkward feeling, you will continue to look around, believing that something just isn't right, no matter how exciting the world seems. Several times, something looks challenging to achieve, but your mind insists that you can make it. It clings to this impossible dream and prompts your body to respond. In a way that you do not expect, your body musters this energy and make your dreams happen.

This is all proof that your mind is a vital piece of you. It is where you find motivation, distraction, support, and depression. Anything that gets to your mind will likely affect the way you think, believe, and react to life. This is why Mahatma Gandhi declares, "I will never let anyone walk through my mind with their dirty feet." In other words, you must never allow any human to sit you down and manipulate you, just so they get what they desire.

Sorrowfully, manipulation of the human mind is the primary mission that some people have set their lives upon. They are the puller of strings and so take delight in pulling any strings that promise to weaken your heart. They also keenly search for the key to your heart, longing to hypnotize you and have you in their pocket. That is, they yearn to have you pretty well under their control. You will fall into many disasters the moment you let them have their way. You would be unable to achieve your goals and longings because they do not tally with theirs.

You have to drop your emotions and displeasure and do just what pleases your exploiters. Some of them even go as far as getting trained in the art of manipulation and exploitation. They read Dark Psychology books so they can learn the art and science of suppression. Remember, whoever has the key to your heart already owns the key to your body, and, virtually, your life.

If you think about your life for just one minute, you'll realize that, at a time or another, you have been manipulated by someone. This person found their way into your heart and made you do what you weren't willing to do from the start. It might have been at home. Probably, your dad, your sister, or your super noisy aunty who struggled to convince you to do something till you agreed. It might have happened at work too. It's probably your boss, colleagues, and partners who forced you to dump your ideas or perspectives and instead subscribe to theirs.

Wherever it was, you'll notice how some of these people are exceptional at it. They can manipulate you, other humans, and anything else that seems possible without much effort. Some had no training in manipulation, but nothing pleases them more than being in control of other people's lives. Even when you try to resist their appeal, your feeble mind feels it has no choice but to eat out of their hands. They win the security and love of others, and they make people helplessly fall in love with them. People even drop their ideas when they listen to these manipulators. I do not desire to mention politicians and business people just yet.

Nevertheless, here is the point where you should wonder, haven't I been manipulated my whole life? Should this really be the reality? Should you manipulate people just to get what you want?

Every human is unique. You are the custodian of your ideas and desires; there is no reason anyone should brainwash you. There is no "why" anyone should quench the burning passion in your mind just to kindle their fire in your heart. Come to think of it, what would happen to all of your childhood dreams and lifelong fantasies if someone manipulated you from this early start of your life? How would you become someone in life if, every day, you had to do the bidding of someone who hypnotized you and coerced you to do only what they wanted? How would the rest of your life seem when you had spent the best part worshipping someone? What would happen to what you want?

Reflect upon it. You are nothing if you cannot have a life of your own. You cannot dream and make things happen on your own. You are not better than computers and machines if, all of your life, you are subjected to someone else or are always craving to manipulate others. This is why you must find yourself a big buckler — you need something vast and terrific that can defend your mind against Dark Psychology for as long as you live.

The world no longer needs Dark Psychology and its proponents. The world needs a different set of spirits and initiatives that can protect them against Dark Psychology and manipulation forever. You need peace, happiness, and to be yourself as you surge through life. You need freedom for your mind, and this is the point where this book will change your life forever.

I have spent the whole of my life battling this reality. Ten thousand Dark Psychology books sit in libraries all over the world, and several thousand more are equally obtained on the internet. You will be shocked to discover how well these books teach manipulation. They teach mistreatment, capitalization, and manipulation of other people's hearts. They show you ways to work yourself into people's backbones and murder their resistance before they even notice. You would be being hypnotized in such a way that you would not even know that you are being manipulated . So how do you get to change the tide? How can you escape from this shackle? How can you find your liberty?

That is what this book will tell you. It is the first weapon against Dark Psychology in the world. It is the first guide that tells you how to handle Dark Psychology. Using the tripartition philosophy, it provides a step by step guide to wriggle yourself out of Dark Psychology class for life. If you have not been wrangled in Dark Psychology, this is the most important book you will need on human relations.

I have detailed ample facts, tips, and realities in such a manner that, no matter where you find yourself or who you find yourself with, you can never be manipulated. Not even natural leaders like your parents, class teachers, or best friends could manipulate you. As long as you do not skip a line in this book, and you follow my proven steps, the sky won't even be enough to manipulate your mind. No matter how you stumbled on this book, I offer my heartiest congratulations. Things will get a little bit theoretical, though I ensure I made everything as practical as possible. All in all, you will be ten steps ahead of every dark psychologist in the world by the time you flip the last page.

This book is structured according to the "Tripartition Theory," which believes that to achieve White Psychology, three factors have to be considered: The Self, The Other, and The Place. The "Self" concerns you. It describes your experiences with psychology and how you can wriggle out of problems like anxiety and emotional tumors. It encompasses information on the fundamental reasons that you fall prey to Dark Psychology, and it lays the foundation for revivification. The first five chapters of this book will show you just that.

Next is the "Other" phase that exposes the flaws of Dark Psychology. Chapter 5 to 10 of this book tells you everything that is not right about Dark Psychology. It shows you how *another* person might attempt to manipulate you and your goals with the ludicrous curls of Dark Psychology. Lastly, the last four chapters complete the tripartition. They open you to the world of White Psychology and hold you by the hand as you tread the path into White Psychology it.

Let's not get too salty about things. Settle in a nice chair and pick your best drink. With undivided attention, flip this page and unravel what I have been talking about.

THE SELF

CHAPTER 1
THE CONCEPT OF WHITE PSYCHOLOGY

White Psychology is one of the finest developments in the world of psychology. It is a form that you would not find in psychology books or libraries because of its newness. You are among the first people to ever read about "White Psychology." You can be sure, however, the notion of it will make it the fastest-growing branch of psychology in the coming years. Its beliefs, notions, and philosophies will make it grow among the most counted on in the world. The tall and short of the world will clamor to apply White Psychology rather than anything else.

Before we get into the nitty-gritty, you must remember that this book is solely written on the tripartition principle. The tripartition principle believes that by considering three wholesome parts, we can get to the bottom of a problem. With this principle, this book is segmented into three: The Self, The Other, and The Place. This chapter and the next four will focus on The Self. You will undoubtedly get to know the instant we veered into The Other and The Place. The Self will provide answers to burning questions about yourself. It will tell you about why you are often a subject of other people's exploitation and it will lay a foundation for your permanent freedom.

So, what exactly is White Psychology?

It's a convoluted form of psychology. You need to understand how exactly it was formed before you can get its full concept. It is the same way "Atkin's, Keto, and so on" would mean nothing unless you know exactly how they came about to be. From the beginning, psychology has been the study of human behavior and is central to our thoughts, actions, and interactions, as Dr. Jason Jones says. It is the study of how our thoughts and actions are linked as humans. Enough psychology can tell you how a human would likely react, given a set of circumstances.

Have you ever wondered what would happen 'if' something else happens? For instance, "What would your uncle say if you tell him you're quitting your job? What would your mom say if she hears that you're moving out of her home for good?" You would find yourself providing a ton of answers to these questions. "She might get mad at me. She might get on her knees and break into tears. She would throw me out and scream that I should never talk to her again," et cetera. By mulling over all of these possibilities, you are actively engaging in psychology. While there are experts who spend all of their lives studying the human mind, it is not insane that you spend some time thinking about other people's minds too. Psychology is the foundation of our thinking cap, and we all are psychologists by default.

Where then does the White come in?

Experts have made an effort to class psychology in different ways. One of these ways is the use of colors. According to this theory, colors can determine the nature of psychology in many cases. In other words, when someone says that you have got a White, Blue, or Dark Psychology, it means something to the experts. Some believe that constant exposure to color might condition your mind in a certain way. We will talk about that in my next book. For now, I earnestly long to focus on White Psychology.

You might be curious, "Okay, Fred, what does white mean in psychology then?" Easy and straightforward. According to the "Color Psychology Organization" in the United Kingdom, white is the perfect emblem for purity, innocence, wholeness, and completion. It is a color that tells the world about meekness, commitment, and unity. It is a symbol of good beginnings, cleanliness, and a spotless start or restart to life. If everything seemed over for you, but you decided to pick yourself up all of a sudden, you are going White. Maybe like someone who died and rose in the middle of their funeral.

White represents balance. It is not particularly attractive, but it balances the spectrum pretty well. It also creates the avenue for whatever a human can conceive in their mind. Babies are the whitest in the world of psychology. They are plain, healthy, unbiased, balanced, and open to all sorts of development. The color "white" certainly holds a lot in the universe of psychology. The amusing thing is that this is not the exact origin of White Psychology.

It is actually a counter-attack. It is a deliberate attempt to fight back, defend, and build upon your own soul against oppressors and manipulators. It is a tactical effort to counter the infamous Dark Psychology, which holds everyone in a bond of some type. White Psychology is a state of the mind that solidly sits that humans should never be manipulated. You must not be cheated, exploited, or hypnotized on any condition.

I choose to define "White Psychology" as the study of the human conditions concerning the psychological nature of people who know how to defend themselves and others against psychic vampires and psychological disturbers that I choose to call Hecklers. Any effort made to manipulate you must be weakened and watered down.

Your friends, parents, or boss must have no right to impose or heap up your life with their unchecked obsessions. You have the power to choose the life of your own. You need to be whole, safe, healthy, and free from the opportunism of people who might take advantage of you. This is the world that White Psychology agitates and seeks to stir up for everyone. In some way, it is not wide apart from the essence of the color white in psychology.

Now that this is all clear, what are "The Foremost Features of White Psychology?"

1. Independence of the human body and soul:

Who deserves to be under the shackles of someone else all through their lives? I don't know if it is just me, but I have never believed that humans are structured to be servants of other people's desires. Each person has a distinct soul, a discrete system, and a distinguishing sense that should be used in their personal relations. Your mind, your beliefs, and your aspirations are different from anyone else's. You are yours to command, and you need to have that independence.

Parents are great people. It is only unnerving that many times they try to weave their ideas into your life. Many parents wish they had been to college and graduated with good grades. They feel they could have had more opportunities if they'd had that education. Some even have professions that they long to take on, but they could not dare. So, they put all their trust in their child to appear and take that career up. They stuff their ambitions in the child's head and expect the child to make it all happen.

Several other parents start a business and expect their child to continue that business, whether the child desires it or not. They want you to see things their way. And they will employ whatever means they can persuade you with. It might not be your own parents in your case. It might be a teacher, a business partner, or anyone.

The obvious fact is that people who manipulate you are likely pretty close to you. No father, mother, friend, or even someone who believes in something different should successfully attempt to put their beliefs in your head. You will learn how to stay on your feet and fight for your dreams through White Psychology.

2. Life dreams actualization

Nothing makes a man feel anguish like unfulfilled dreams. It creates a hole in your heart, a longing that spreads pain beyond what your words can ever tell anyone. If you crave a career, a job, or a life partner, you will never feel accomplished until this dream is arched into reality. It is just as Seth David Chernoff says: "The loss of life is not nearly as devastating as the loss of what could have been, of the dreams left unfulfilled and lingering passions undiscovered."

There are two ways you can remember how this feels. Pause for a minute, shut your eyes, and think about that one thing you desperately desired in your life that you never got. Outside that, remember to ask your grandpa how it feels to have dreams that one could not fulfill.

Through Dark Psychology, several dreams will never be fulfilled. Several aspirations will never be accomplished, and a countless number of people will live in pain all through their lives. It is precisely what White Psychology is putting up a fight against. People should never have to quit their dreams to fulfill someone else's. There is no life without a dream. Neither is a life worth something when its aspirations are not achieved. To stress this point, Carl Jung, once said, "The dream is the small hidden door in the deepest and most intimate sanctum of the soul..."

3. **Empathy and support**

Empathy refers to the compassionate ability to understand other people. It refers to the tender warmness with which you generate people's love without manipulating them. It is what happens when you can see through people's pains and be sympathetic to them. It does not matter what people's positions are or seem like to you. As long as you are empathetic, you will be able to understand each other without exploiting each other.

For Dark psychologists, empathy is an overused method of exploitation. The Dark psychologists prompt their prey with lies and deceit to the point where these victims feel emotional about them. Their victims become hypnotized and feel compelled to do the bidding of their hecklers.

Your number one examples are the friends who told you lies of many kinds so that you can hand some of your cash to them. It is the same thing your mom does just to ensure that you get emotional and champion her cause. Your boss, your colleagues, staffers, and even opponents will use this trick so that you can feel empathetic with them. It is all clear proof of exploitation. With White Psychology, however, you are bound to be empathetic with each other. It is only that you do not feel each other's pains so you could hurt each other. Instead, you make efforts to support each other. No one ever exploits the other.

4. **Protection against manipulation**

The most significant emphasis of White Psychology has been on manipulation. It insists that each human should be allowed to grow, choose their life, and go after their respective desires without interference from anyone. You and everyone else should not be compelled to live a life because someone else thinks it is right for you. Your mind also has to be free of subjection and interference.

If someday, an award should be dished out to a branch of psychology that protects the human mind, White Psychology would fit the bill to a tee. Adopting White Psychology would mean that, for the rest of your life, you will never exploit unsuspecting humans. You will remain fierce in your constant fight against the manipulation of the mind. You will never be used by people who simply want to get something out of you. You will not be suppressed by people who want to be made your priority. And, at all times, you will be guarded against manipulation.

History gets into making at all times — people remember who was with them in their yesteryears, and they realized how much manipulation came from them from the start. Then, they come after you or your generation in retaliation. It is never a thrilling experience to be hunted in the later years of your life. It will not happen to you with White Psychology; you will neither become the oppressor nor the oppressed.

5. **A world free from deceit**

As pointed out by the Merriam Webster Dictionary, deceit is the act of causing someone to accept as correct or valid what is false or invalid. It is the deliberate act of telling people things that are not true or persuading them to accept fallacies so that you can have your way. It is what you do when you do not want people to see the truth, when you want to maneuver their mind away from getting the hang of a situation.

Deceit is a common trend in the modern world. People far and near you will try to deceive you. Sellers, business people, and politicians at all levels will appeal to iotas of deceit to earn your votes. You will also grow up to realize that, right from the start of your life, your parents had deceived you about Santa Claus and several other fairy tale stories.

If you look into these lies with a transparent and open heart, you will realize that the lies all center around the same point — every one of your manipulators was trying to make you see things in a certain way. They were trying to make you believe things the way it pleased them, and not according to reality. But the instant high and low people subscribe to White Psychology jingles all over the world, you'll recognize a new hope, a new light, and a world practically free of deceits.

6.   **All-encompassing   anti-Dark Psychology:**

Dark Psychology is the symbol of every wrong thing in human interaction. It is the symbol of extortion, and it represents inequality and injustice. It is the perfect way you can explain how people could cheat on others and trick them of what they have. You identify the weakness of other people and subconsciously rip them of their natural privileges, whether they did you wrong at any point or not. Dark Psychology stresses that there should be no forgiveness of other people's shortcomings. You should only take it out on whoever looks like a ready victim. It stands for greed, being overzealous, a lack of contentment, and sheer disregard for the fundamental right of humans. Controlling the mind of others for your gain is as bad as enslaving them — perhaps worse.

Your only solace is that you can protect yourself against manipulation at a moderate level. If all of these continue to exist in the interaction of the human race, there is no telling how much they could affect humanity. It implies that humans will always be on their toes so that they can hurt and cheat other people, and that they will forever struggle to remain in control.

7. Absence of manipulation or hypnosis

How would the world look if there was no manipulation at all? There are no fantabulous Santa stories. There are no weird fairy dreams, and "forever and ever" fancies are not concocted. Your business partners tell you things as they are, and your parents distinguish what they desire from what they do, leaving the decision all in your hands. Your siblings, friends, and associates make no effort to trick, double-cross, or pull a fast one on you when you're not looking.

Beyond the shores, politicians and influential citizens remain true to what they say. They stand for what they indeed believe. There are no sly games from everyone at any time. Your friend is your friend, and your foe is, undoubtedly, your foe. Anyone who tells you that they have deep feelings for you is genuinely in love with you. Without sways or magic, you can completely believe what people say. A world like this sounds too perfect to be true — it does not seem to have loops and shortcomings of any type. Yet, it is entirely achievable if people were to learn to stick their efforts at the right angle.

8. The self-discovery game

Discovering yourself is key to living a life of prosperity and happiness. Life has close to no meaning if you cannot make head or tail of what to do with yourself. You do not have any idea of the stuff you are made up of, and all you earnestly want to do is figure out what would gratify your heart. As a famous philosopher notes, two days are the most important in your life — the day you were birthed, and the day you find out why.

There are several reasons that you find it super hard to discover the stuff you are made of, and one of the top reasons is manipulation. Over the years, you have been told different lies and inconsistencies just to suit a particular situation. Your mom has told you several times that you seem good at baking. And she might be right, except she said that so you do not feel bad about your baking skills. She could have told you to never try cooking.

Probably, you might be better at something else. These deliberate and indeliberate manipulations all contribute to your lack of growth. You have to shake off deceits of people from your mind and ace the space!

Tips To Remember

1. Humanity needs to fight manipulation with full force.

2. Dark Psychology is a disaster in the existence of humanity.

3. You need to fight for your independence and chase your dreams through White Psychology.

CHAPTER 2
CONFESSIONS OF A FORMER ANXIETY VICTIM

Close this book.

Reach for your mobile, call anyone and fire the question, "What is anxiety?" You will discover in one minute that the whole world seems to have an idea of what anxiety is about. Someone thinks that anxiety makes one nervous and uncomfortable. Another person says it gets in your heart and make you troubled, restless, and unsettled, whether there is a reason or not. We all know that anxiety can make people react in strange and unusual ways. You will hear all that as you make the calls.

However, there is a stark reality that most people don't know about anxiety — it grants the ultimate password to exploitation from other people. It is one way that Dark psychologists can get into people's hearts without limits or conditions. Already, we have hinted that Dark Psychology is a deliberate attempt to get into someone's heart and force them to do only what pleases them. Let's piece it together now.

A person's anxiety is the fastest medium through which Dark psychologists can penetrate and subsequently acquire their hearts. If you get very anxious about something and a heckler picks up the scent, it would be straightforward to get into your spirit and win you over. The objective of this book is to render you free from the shackles of Dark Psychology, so we will spend most of this chapter listening to the firsthand experience of Ken — a former victim of anxiety. But before that, we will try to understand the exact definition of anxiety and its implications.

What exactly is anxiety?

According to Kimberly Holland, "Anxiety is the human's natural reaction to stress. It is a feeling of fear and apprehension about what might happen soon." Anxiety is our body's way of showing that we are scared, nervous, or in an uncertain situation. When you are anxious, you might feel some crinkles in your tummy and some lumps down your throat. You almost feel alive and dead in a single minute: your heart pulses very fast and wild, and if the feeling is extreme enough you may suffer a panic attack. The body reacts in several ways that cannot all be listed; you might have all of these symptoms or just a few.

Being anxious about what is about to happen is acceptable. It makes you conscious of yourself and your environment. It helps your body respond to danger, since your body takes in the signs and gets itself prepared for action. Typically, you will not get anxious about everything — you only get anxious about certain aspects of your life. For instance, you might be anxious about your job, future, security, life partner, or kids, among others. Once you are worried about anyone, your body will show nervousness, discomfort, and some signs of anxiety each time you talk or think about that thing you're anxious about.

It is easy to tell when someone has a migraine, typhoid, or even cholera. They can tell a doctor how they feel, and the doctor can guess what prompted it and the best medication in a minute. In the case of anxiety, you are faced with a different situation. No one knows exactly how to describe their feelings. What's more, anything in the world can trigger anxiety. You could be anxious over the dress you wear to a ball, as perhaps, you feel it doesn't look charming or attractive. You could be worried about how you will perform in your new job, or the crazy deadlines you have ahead.

In any case, nobody understands how much you feel when you are anxious, especially when you have no proof, and instead all that you have is feelings about things. "Oh, I get it. But you should relax, it's going to be fine!" Your friends and family think that you shouldn't be worried about whatever makes you anxious. So, they try to talk light of it and play it down. Has that ever happened to you? I will show you an instance from Ken's life in the next few lines. Ken is a young man that I met in Kansas. He was giving up on life when we met at a restaurant. I told him about White Psychology and he instantly decided to adopt it for the rest of his life. He narrated some of his life's ordeals that spurred from anxiety, and you will read it all in this chapter.

The only people who quickly understand your feelings are psychologists and very close relatives. The only saddening reality is that people who understand us can easily manipulate our emotions. The instant they spot the hole in your heart, they try to fill the vacuum and penetrate your heart through it. They see it as a secret alleyway into your heart a take advantage of it before you begin to suspect (you will also find an example of this in Ken's story). Psychic hecklers are like psychologists — they study your mind, and try to understand how the mind works. Do not forget.

Here is a simple analogy you will remember. While growing up, you probably had bad dreams at some point and told your parents. In turn, your parents might have told you tales about how angels are near to protect you, or how fairies are out in the wind to look after you. Sometimes, it is about how there is someone or something out there trying to hurt you, so you should not go out to play in the dark. The story can go in a million ways. The point is that your parents knew that you were anxious about something and seized that moment to manipulate your mind and got their way. Can you remember the version of these fairy tales that you were told?

**"Anxiety in my family and college life."
—Ken**

Ken is my name, and I am from the state of Kansas in the U.S. I am twenty-six now, but the story began when I was six years old, give or take. I grew up as a younger child in my home, with Mike, my older brother. We started life with our mom and dad, and we were never separated from them all through our growth. There were no grannies and nannies around — it was just the family and me. We were a beautiful little family, except that dad and mom never returned early from work. We did all the chores ourselves since our home was a small cape cod that could be easily taken care of. And everyone was fine.

Giant trees like the Custer Elm and Osage coated several streets in our city. They surrounded several houses, too, including ours. They were so huge that I felt like a little toy beside them, and I try to avoid staring up when I would walk under them. One actually looked like it would fall over your head and crush you when you walked under it.

On winter nights, the wind was fierce, and it often made the trees whirl right and left. The trees would whistle strange sounds all over the houses as they waved to the wind's rhythm. I was six. I had no idea why there was often a strange sound on cold and stormy nights. I didn't know about night chills and all. I heard the whistles of the chilling breezes, and I tried to ask my parents about them.

"Mom, what's that? Is it coming here?" My parents knew that I loved night sightseeing, and they badly wanted me in bed by 8 o'clock. They hated returning around 10 o'clock to see that Mike and I were not in the house. So, they grabbed that chance and told me that there was a monster out on the street. "It comes out on cold nights, and it is ready to eat kids up. If it catches you roaming the streets at night, it might tear you to shreds and eat you up."

I shuddered in fear. I fell into agoraphobia and never went into the woods at night, whether there was a storm or not. But the possibility sparked my curiosity. "How could a monster eat anyone up?" I didn't know. And I wasn't sure I wanted to die trying to understand. I tucked myself in bed with thoughts of the monster. *Why does it eat kids? Why does it appear just at night?*

I had many questions that I wanted to figure out. My spine tingled each time my parents talked about it. "It is bigger than a gorilla, and it has an ugly head like an Australia snake." And so on it went — there was always a new detail about the monster. I didn't ask them any more questions. I didn't want my friends to take the mickey out of me, so I didn't ask them either. I found myself looking around the woods each time I walked by, in case the monster was just taking a nap nearby or peering at me.

Now and then, I could feel the monster's eyes on my skin. It left a knuckle in my stomach that I wished I could tear apart. I could almost feel the monster walking right behind me when I walked. But I didn't dare look over my shoulders. Sometimes, I trembled and vomited all over wherever I pictured that image. My parents triggered a generalized anxiety disorder in me — anxiety about survival and security. I had no idea what was going to happen if the monster caught me. So, I kept to Michael's side each time I walked by the trees.

Michael knew that I was terrified by the monster, and he took advantage of that too. He told me that the beast was fierce-looking, and it had eaten up many kids that he knew. But he was willing to protect me with some special powers that he had. I only had to give up whatever was in my lunch pack when we got to school. I felt I had no choice. I agreed, and Mike had my lunch pack all the time. From that age, Mike didn't stop having my lunch until I turned fifteen. I grew thin and sick, and the thought of this monster cluttered my dreams as I stared at the huge trees around the house every day. I developed chronic anxiety.

As if that wasn't enough, I got anxious during college too. I was warming up for college by fifteen, and I had learned enough to realize that there are no monsters in the night whirls. It was just that I still heard fast, pounding beats in my heart each time the wind blew north. And as I left home for college, I began to get nervous over some different set of problems. My anxieties included the following:

- **Social Anxiety**

Social Anxiety happens when a person becomes worried about how they will fit into the society that they find themselves. They are wondering what the community thinks of them or if they are fit to be in society. It is an anxiety that pulls you apart from the crowd. It makes you avoid speaking in public, avoid making friends, and so on. You often get social anxiety when you move to a new environment. When I left home for the University of Saint Mary, social anxiety was my starting problem — I had no idea what was right or wrong in the community. I wasn't sure how brilliant students should dress, or the elite views of certain aspects of life. I tried to get out of everyone's way because I wasn't sure of how excited they would be to become my friends. It was a world way different from my little home in Kansas.

- **Peer Anxiety**

As I struggled to fit into society, another anxiety I developed was peer anxiety. I felt nervous and timid among people who should be my peers. They were high profile students who had wealth and seemed super intelligent. I was an average student who got into Saint Mary on a supplementary list. I clumsily wondered how I would cope among these students and felt awfully intimidated. I never uttered a word in the lecture halls. I didn't try to make friends, and I worked hard to never bump into anyone so that they wouldn't make fun of me. I merely attended the classes and flew off the second class was over.

- **Test Anxiety**

Test Anxiety is a common disorder in the classroom. It is a type of anxiety that makes you scared of tests. It makes you wonder what your tests will be like and how you will perform. When you eventually sit to write the test, test anxiety can make you nervous during the trial. It might make you uncomfortable, tense, and worried all through. I was struck by this anxiety several times. I made all sorts of errors while anxiously trying to do something fantastic. The worst of all,

I would be done with my exams and couldn't help thinking about what my scores would be.

- **Job Performance**

You feel job performance anxiety when you land the best job of your life. You realize it is a golden opportunity, and you earnestly long to ensure that you make no mistakes with it. You either do your best or do your best. You would likely be more anxious if you had no experience. When I left college and got a job at 22, I was hired on trial by the manager. He warned that I had no experience, but I would have to gel into the system as soon as possible. He would not tolerate underperformance, and I might get fired any moment he decided it. This kept me on my toes at all times.

- **My partner's feelings**

In case no one has told you, seventeen to thirty is the most sensitive age bracket. It is the age where you have to start many things in your life and blend them. It is the period during which you feel the highest level of uncertainty about everything. When you fall in love with someone and make them your life partner, you sometimes find yourself wondering how they really feel. *Does he love me? Can he see what is going through my mind? Does he feel the way that I do?* Fears that your partner probably doesn't love you might cloud your thoughts and unsettle you once in a while.

Effects in my life

1. Constant fear:

No thanks to my family's insincerity, I lived most of my adolescent life in fear and insecurity. I never shut my eyes in my bed without thinking of a human-eating monster. My heart thumped fiercely each time I stepped into the streets, and I was always watching my back. I trembled when the cloudy weather looked dull. I spent my early life on the lookout for something that was non-existent. I was running from nothing!

2. Insecurity

Insecurity does not necessarily imply that there is something intent on shooting you down. Insecure feelings begin when something in your heart feels like you are not entirely safe. It happens when everywhere looks calm, serene, and secure. Yet, you can feel troubling and uncomfortable emotions deep in your skin. In my case, I felt dizziness, nausea, and I often doubled over without stumbling on anything. Sometimes, I jumped when anyone touched me, and I never stopped wondering if someone was lurking around to hurt me.

3. Poor psychological growth

Your psychological growth is as vital as your physical growth. If you have been anxious your whole life, you will likely not have balanced mental growth. Remember what I said about myself as I turned fifteen: "I realized that there was no monster in the woods by then. But I still felt the fast and loud thumps of my heartbeat each time thunderclapped in the sky." This is a pointer to how much anxiety can damage your psychological growth. Your brain could be conditioned to certain psychological situations for life. It was no different at school. I felt inferior, scared, and uncomfortable when everyone else was excitedly chatting around me.

4. Prey to psychic hecklers

The most damaging effect of anxiety is that it rendered me prey to psychic hecklers. I became vulnerable to unchecked psychologists, who realized my weak spot and used it to veer into my heart. As a handy illustration, Mike knew that I was scared of monsters that didn't exist. He behaved like a typical psychic heckler by manipulating my mind to believe my illusions were real, when, instead, he could have clarified my uncertainties. Moreover, he acted like an average heckler when he exploited my emotional deficiency so that he could get what he desired: my lunch pack.

Is anxiety so difficult to hack? Let's see!

Tips To Remember

1. People close to you have a higher chance of manipulating you than anyone else.

2. You can be exploited through what you are anxious about.

3. There are different forms of anxiety.

4. Anxiety can have damaging effects in your life.

CHAPTER 3
HACKING ANXIETY SHOULD BE STUPIDLY EASY FOR YOU

We spent all of the last chapter talking about anxiety and its depth in our individual lives. We have made it clear that not only can anxiety wreck you, it can also make you vulnerable to people who are dying. This is why hacking your fear should be top on your bucket list. Interestingly, hacking anxiety is stupidly easy for everyone. If you didn't think that way, it is because you haven't realized how effortless it could be. Not to worry, I am going to show you the simplest way to hack anxiety in the next few lines. If you knew some ways earlier, trust me, my suggestions are more straightforward than the most uncomplicated method you have ever seen. Ready to journey through them? Let's do it!

Comfy ways to ease anxiety

1. Create an emergency pack

You need an emergency pack many times throughout your life. It is not just when you get into a marathon or when something knocks you unconscious — you need an emergency pack when you are battling anxiety too. You are going to agree that anxiety is a full-time business. Once you are anxious about anything, you will think about it now and then. As an illustration, let's say you have been anxious about your son's health. He was acting weird all day, and you didn't understand. If you try to focus on solving a task or cracking a code at work, you might find yourself distracted by thinking about your boy then too. Your attention would drift now and then, and it would be impossible to concentrate. If you were anxious over your love life, your career, or anything, it would all reflect in that same manner. This is enough proof that anxiety will apprehend you now and then.

In preparation for the next time, you should create an emergency pack. What is that? A bag of activities, thoughts, and reactions that can completely take your mind off whatever makes you anxious. You should think about something that you know pretty well that will bring your mind off your anxiety for good if you consider it. Some examples are the tasks you left last week, or the debate you will have over the coming week. In another case, you might pick your phone and dial your friends mobile. Once you realize that you are battling anxiety, create an emergency pack, and act it out the next time you feel anxious; you will be impressed with yourself.

2. **Reserve some "worry time"**

This is something you will hardly ever hear from anyone. Yet, it is one of the simplest and most effective methods of fixing anxiety. You need to have a "worry time" — a period that you set aside in the day only to think. It is a period that you turn your phone off, shut off the TV, and sever the Wi-Fi just so that you can concentrate on your inner self. To use your worry time efficiently, you should sit somewhere and think about your troubling issues. Your objective is to ponder over some disconcerting questions and find lasting solutions to them.

To prepare for this moment, you should ensure your preferred location is as quiet as possible. You should have no friends over, no noise, and no music except if you are addicted to thinking with music. You also want to prepare a list of the life snags that you desire to find a solution to. When all of these are set, you should settle down and ease your nerves as much as possible. Then try to think extensively on a problem. Shut your eyes and relax as you think about each one. You should also try to ensure that you do not think about anything else other than this problem. Think so objectively that you would see the cons and pros of the snags, and why and how you can put an end to it. Do all of that on a problem before getting to the next one. Remember to do your meditation in a moment that you won't have to run off to work, catch an appointment, or do anything else. The world has to be out for now. It's just you!

If you have a moment like this, you should be able to solve your problems more creatively. You should also be able to handle your problems better since you approach them with thorough thinking. Not to forget, your resolutions on a problem should be penned down from the resolution room. You do not have to fix a meditation hour every day. It might be as frequent as three times in a week, or one or two more.

Whatever makes you anxious should be penned down and reserved until your meditation hour. Your body will likely choose to relax a little bit more on the problem, once it knows pretty well that all of its worries will be hashed out at some point soon. Rather than remain anxious, it will likely keenly look forward to the meditation hour instead.

3. **Pick the points**!

What is the lesson to be picked from all of these problems? Look deeply. A famous philosopher says that, "Every experience in life comes with a lesson." If you do not learn that lesson, you will likely repeat the experience. This is one top reason you should focus on getting the points out of your experiences. Like my friend, have you fallen in love with someone you can't possibly go to? It is a clue that it is possible to fall in love with someone else after this individual. What might keep you firm is your resolution to stick to your family.

Are you getting anxious about your clouded schedule and the life-threatening demands of your boss? It is probably a clue that you are underperforming, and you have to step up your game. It might also equally be a hint that it is time to switch your job. Whatever made you feel anxious is passing a message to you. When you focus on picking out the point, you will naturally become less anxious. You have seen a positive side to your anxiety, and its negativity seems to be watered down. What are you worried about? Don't let it go without picking the points! *"Look at your problems, and they will continue to hold you down. See them as blessings in disguise, and that is what they truly become."* — Dalai Lama.

4. Source the opposite emotion

Anxiety is a feeling that makes you tremble all the way down your spine. It makes you feel that everything is slipping away right before your eyes, and you can do nothing to hold it together. It makes you doubt your talent and your ability to handle many situations, most especially ones that you have never handled before. The fact that a situation is new does not make it impossible for you to feel, it only implies that it requires you to think differently. If you are anxious about it, you can't possibly get it right! This is why you need to find the opposite emotion to anxiety.

You need to be confident. You have to be self-motivated and positive in your subconscious thoughts. There are several ways you can make this happen. One of the most common ways is to use a mantra. Mantras are short and simple quotes that you repeat to yourself often. I will extensively tell you how that works in the next chapter. Apart from mantras, you may turn to listening to motivational quotes from successful people. It feels good to know that there is someone who has been in your shoes or something similar, and they were able to scale through. If you are not using a motivational speaker or mantras to calm your anxiety, you could try music.

Several people have a song or two that they listen to when their emotions are heavy and they do not feel up to things. It works pretty well for them as they hum the songs. If you have got a song that you have a fondness for, you should try listening to it during your anxious moments. If it isn't music, maybe drama, artworks, or a walk down the avenue, the riverside, or anywhere else that you believe could calm your anxiety might work.

5. You need an emotion library

As the Germans say, "A problem shared is half solved." If you can read and write, you have no idea how powerful you are —you can solve half of your problems without calling anyone. All you need to do is pick up your pen and put down all of your problems. You would be shocked to realize that, as you put down your problems, it becomes lighter in your heart; as if you have found a solution. As it works for every other problem, it works for anxiety too. You can fix your anxiety by having a journal where you write down your emotional outbursts each time you have them. If you had a persistent anxiety attack recently, it would be a brilliant idea to go about with writing it down. Rather than become a recipient of your perplexing emotions, you will soon turn yourself to the intermediary. You will transfer the feelings from your mind where the emotion sprouts to the book that receives all of the emotional downpour. That way, you will be minimally affected when you would have carried the full weight. Isn't that fantastic?

You do not even have to try out all of these methods. Just one is enough to quell your anxiety, but trying more than one is acceptable, nonetheless. What do you feel anxious about? Which of the methods should work better for you?

If this works for anxiety, let's discuss emotions in general!

Tips to remember

1. You can effortlessly hack anxiety,
2. These five ways can make it happen for you:
    a. Create an emergency pack
    b. Pick the points!
    c. Source the opposite emotion
    d. Use an emotion library
    e. Reserve some "worry time"

CHAPTER 4
3 SOLID WAYS TO CONTROL YOUR EMOTIONS

"When dealing with people, remember that you are not dealing with creatures of logic, but with creatures of emotion."

– Dale Carnegie

Emotion is from the Latin word "emovere." It means to agitate, trigger, or move something. It is used in English to represent a state when the mind is stirred up towards something. When you get emotional, you feel angry, excited, scared, and so forth about something. You also feel an undying instinct about something, coupled with physiological reactions. Emotion is one of the most significant features that separate humans from other inhabitants of the earth. It is your ability to feel, to believe, and to firmly hold on to things that you cannot see or touch — remember a time when you had no proof or clue of any kind, but you still had a strong feeling in your gut about something?

One mysterious fact about emotion is that it is not reliable. Many times, you would have an impulse that seems strong and convincing to you. You could strongly feel that someone was lying or something terrible was going to happen. You would believe it, of course, and you would try to make someone else understand. There is, however, no guarantee that what you felt is indeed right. The person might turn out to be correct, and nothing might happen, and In that way, you be would totally wrong despite the strength of your instincts.

On the flip side, it might also turn out that your feeling was right. You had no proof, and you had no weapon other than your instincts, but at the end of the day, it turned out that you were right. Both situations can happen. The real question is, how do we recognize whether an emotion is correct or not? How can we be sure that the impulse you feel this time is true or not? You should remember that being right about something yesterday offers no guarantee that you will be right again tomorrow.

All of that leaves us in a tight spot — there is no surefire way to gauge whether an emotion is real, untrue, moderate, or inadequate.

Another interesting thing is that what makes you happy might make the next person upset. You felt inspired by what a motivational speaker said, but the person right beside you felt irritated and demotivated. This has nothing to do with the quality of the utterance. Someone else still might get inspired, even if the speaker used foul or cruel language. So, emotions can trigger different reactions from people in the same situation. It can also trigger similar reactions. There is just no one way to measure it. Apart from that, we cannot prove whether a feeling about a situation is good, bad, proper, or improper.

Emotion is a natural law of human existence. Whether you like it or not, you will get emotional about several things. You will become excited, feel in love, be uncomfortable, and feel all sorts about almost everything. The same way you think about objects and people, you will have emotions about them. For instance, you could naturally feel that someone is horrible, or attractive, and so on before you even get to know a lot about them. That is nothing. The real deal is that emotion can wax so strong that what you feel will sometimes overrule what you think when you make decisions.

In other words, you could have some fine research reports which state that heading north or doing a particular thing might be a bad idea. Yet, your emotions firmly cling to this "bad idea," and you will likely make the final decisions based on what you feel rather than what the facts say. Have you been in that type of situation? It is what happens when you choose the last seat on the public bus or train when the chair nearest to the door is vacant. Your thinking would have explained that a nearer position means a quicker exit with getting to your destination, but your emotion insists that you head straight to the last chair on the bus. These silent battles happen each time we make decisions, and emotions often win.

This is what Dale Carnegie implies when he says, "When dealing with people, remember that you are not dealing with creatures of logic, but with creatures of emotion." It is also proof that emotion holds a higher rank than common sense in human psychology. As humans, we will never feel accomplished until we listen to our feelings and refuse to apply contrasting common sense. There is a point to emphasize at this moment — emotion is not a neutral tingling. It can be pleasant or unpleasant, and it can result in both good and bad situations.

Typically, harmful or unpleasant emotions inspire doubt, anger, and uncertainty about a situation. They might also make you feel uneasy over something when it is not harmful or dangerous in any way. Take anxiety as a practical illustration. When you get too anxious about something, you might suffer a panic attack and lose your mental balance. You might begin to sweat excessively or tremble. You might feel chest pain, and completely disappear into your thoughts, withdrawn from your environment. None of that sounds healthy for you.

By the way, unpleasant emotions are weaknesses that a heckler can spot a mile away. A mind heckler is an overzealous person who wants you to see things their way. To win, they try to see things the way you see it first and cloak you when you are not looking. For instance, let's say you were trembling because your lover just left you, and I have been asking you for something which you denied all the while. I could show up and tell you, "Hey, here is some tea. What if I can help you get revenge on your partner, and I could still get you someone better?" You would likely say yes, and you would provide whatever I want. That is it, I win — the psychic heckler wins.

You will soon understand how mind hecklers manipulate people and situations when we discuss them in the next phase. For now, you need to know how to control your emotions. You need to know how to keep things in check so that your feelings will not render you prey to people who are looking to subjugate you and make you live your life just for them. Here and now, I will introduce:

Three solid ways to control your emotions

1. Doing the mental math
2. Hitting the self-control button
3. Source for the opposite emotion

1. Doing the mental math

Mental math is a deliberate effort to reason out the reality of a situation. It is an attempt to understand why certain things happen. It is you racking your brain to figure out why your emotions are heading a certain way and how you can keep them in check. You can have your mental math focused on a feeling that is becoming too strong in your heart. Basically, it implies that you count the options you have, reason out the problems, and try to figure out a solution.

As you have figured out in the previous section, emotion is a psychological situation that has no proof in the outer world. You cannot tell whether what is happening in your head can cling to proof on the outside. You also do not know whether your gut would be proved right, proper, or improper over time. So, whatever is happening in your mind is an inner battle that has to be fought and won. This makes mental math the perfect show to the rescue.

Think about Ken and yourself. You have been manipulated your whole life because you didn't do the mental math. If Ken had tried to douse his fears before asking his parents what was running outside, they would never have told him there was a monster. If you had handled the break up from your partner pretty well, I would never have seen your emotions to the point that I could manipulate them to get what I want. So, mental math is necessary to permanently protect yourself from your friends, colleagues, and people around you who are waiting to get into you through your weakness.

Here are some mental exercises that you can try to work on for your mental math surrounding an emotion:

a. Label the feeling

One of the primary ways to start your mental math is to painstakingly label the feeling. You need to clearly understand, recognize, and identify this feeling. You cannot fix a problem or set it right if you are unsure about what it is. So, you must learn to label the feeling before anything else. If you are not sure what the feeling is yet, then you need to pay more attention to it.

When you label a feeling, you are making efforts to describe that feeling in clear and precise terms. You are trying to ensure that you understand the sensitivity of this emotion in earnest. You want to say, "I am feeling anxious about what will happen in court tomorrow," or, "I am scared of what he might say if I tell him that I love him." Et cetera.

Doing this is vital, because emotion is not always straightforward. Sometimes you might feel that you are happy only to look deeply into yourself and realize you are sad about the situation. You might think the feeling is confidence when, in reality, every fiber of you is getting anxious about something. You may even laugh when you are sad. You may also choose to cry to express your happiness. And let's not talk about the times that you have a mixed reaction about a situation. It is pretty clear that emotion can sit up in the air of confusion. So, you need to look deep beyond your façade and name your real feelings.

b. Question it severely

Having recognized your current emotions, you should press it further with more questions. These will help you realize the value of this emotion to your soul. You will have a realistic idea of which of your feelings are truly important to the world. You will also catch it when things are going overboard, as long as your questions are entirely objective. You should not presume that you know — instead, put the questions to yourself with an open mind.

As starting questions, you should query about "How do I feel right now?" According to Bruce Lee, a Forbes analyst, humans can feel no less than 27 emotions. Here are the common ones:

You could be amused, anxious, bored, calm, envious, excited, scared, horrified, happy, in love, interested, sympathetic, lusty, romantic, adoring, appreciating aesthetics, in awe, confused, and disgusted. Having identified whatever it is, you can continue to the next phase:

Why do I feel like this? What triggered it?

There is a range of reasons you could feel emotions about something. It is entirely up to you to look around and find your answers to it. On getting to know why or what triggered it, you need to see if it is worth it. Is it fine? Is it going to hurt some other people? Is this the path to self-destruction and humiliation? So, is it worth it? All of that can give you a strong clue to your next phase. This phase is where you wonder whether you are becoming prey to psychic hecklers or whether you are treading off the path of common sense. It is crucial to be objective all along. If you are not objective, you may not answer in all sincerity, and you might generate the wrong answers. If you are objective, however, you must have been faced with some fierce realities already.

c. Creatively think about the alternatives

Now that you know exactly where your feelings might land you, it will be useful to consider alternatives. Would it happen if there is a better option lurking around? Should you espouse or suppress your emotions? You should equally try to introduce whatever emotions you have chosen into your system subconsciously. For instance, if you were feeling anxious earlier and you have decided to wipe it off with confidence, then wear your confidence! Make it clear to your system that you have to be confident about your situations and replace your anxiety as soon as possible.

d. Consider the effects

One last thing. This is not a straight line solution — it is cyclical. This is not something that ends after you have introduced a new emotion into your system. It is a process that continues, and you have to keep evaluating. Just like you considered the first emotion, you need to keep evaluating the other alternatives you have as well. *Is this working for my system? Does it express what I honestly believe or what I am trying to make the world feel? Is this perfect?*

Right now, something in my gut tells me that you have fallen in love with the mental math method already, right? But don't get too excited, it isn't even the end. There are two others. Let's see them!

2. **Hitting the self-control button**

The self-control button is the most important in the human system. It is one button that makes you entirely different from every other species of living things on Earth. You should understand that there is no such literal button; it is just a figurative expression. It is an attempt to explain that your ability to control yourself is the most exclusive feature of humans. No lower animal or plant can control itself so much that it can manage its internal and external situations without a glitch. But, good thing for you, you're one of the species that can do it. And it's best that you do it when it comes to emotion.

Typically, it is not easy to tell when your emotion is going overboard — T when you are starting to feel too much of something. Yet, you should make every effort to monitor how you are expressing a specific emotion. Let me ask you a question: Have you ever visited someone and bought a particular type of flower because the whole world knows that they love that flower? Good! It might not be flowers in your case. It might just be that you are trying to win someone over, and you bought the exact thing that the whole world knew they wouldn't do without. Has it ever happened? Great!

The first point is that this person has no control over their desires. They forgot to use their control button on their desires, so much that what their love is a medium through which the high and low of psychic hecklers (you included) can penetrate them.

On the flip side, have you ever been confused about a special gift to offer someone because you are not sure what to buy them? It is not just you. No one seems to have an idea of what they love and what they do not. Has that happened once? It implies that this person is self-controlled to the point that you cannot clearly tell what they want from what they have no interest in. It does not mean that they do not have desires. In reality, every person in the world has a soft spot for something, whether you have noticed or not. Some are just conscious enough to realize it and hide it, so it doesn't become their open weak spot. This is precisely what I desire to emphasize in this chapter.

You need to protect yourself from Dark psychologists permanently. You need to hide that part that can be used to waggle their way into you. People's children are stolen because of the kidnappers' realization that they have a keen love for their child. Trust me. If you love your child and you are able to mask it so well, your child can't be a case in point for enemies to battle you. You need freedom, and you need to hide your weak spots.

So, what are the steps to controlling your emotions?

a. Balance with logic

In plain words, logic is the science of thinking about things objectively before making a decision. It emphasizes that you should consider all facts and figures before choosing. The number one way to avert disheartening situations is to balance your emotions with logic at all times.

You must try to ensure that you are not merely emotional about something — you have to be able to think things through and justify it. Before you stand up to object to what Mrs. Bell said in the boardroom, ask yourself, have I got points? Am I merely up because she hates me for no reason and would not accept my advances? Before you quit your job because you don't like it, have you found a better job? You need logic to work side by side with your emotions. *"For how do we know that two and two make four? Or that the force of gravity works? Or that the past is unchangeable? If both the past and the external world exist only in mind, and if the mind itself is controllable..."* — George Orwell

b. Use a Mantra

As Kelsey Patel says, "A mantra is a word, prayer, or sound vibration that is repeated to create a state of concentration, consciousness, and connection." A mantra is a phrase or clause which you generate with the sole objective of communicating with your subconscious mind. By subconscious mind, I mean the voice that lives inside your mind and tells you things. It gives you decisions based on how it feels and tempts you to do several things.

Your subconscious mind can be your most excellent motivator, and it can also bring down your spirits more than anything in the world. If it feels like you are going to be poor, miserable, and unlovable for the rest of your life, there is a slim chance that you will be otherwise. The number one reason is that the subconscious mind speaks to you at all times; it repeats its beliefs to you every second. It makes you doubt that you can step out of its limitations even when you clearly can. "It is wrong! This is not you!" it would scream in your head when you try to step out of its beliefs. This is why you cannot change anything on the outside if it is not something that your subconscious agrees with.

In the words of Karol Ward, "A morning mantra can change how you feel about yourself, which is the most important thing to change." Hence, it becomes important to apply mantras in your life dealings. In practice, simple words, quotes, and illustrations can suffice as mantras. You can make up each morning and tell yourself, "I am going to be objective. I will not judge by my emotions," and so on. Gradually, your subconscious mind takes this in and warns you that you should not judge by your emotions, and you have promised to be objective each time you are about to make a decision.

3. Search for the opposite emotion

As I have suggested in the previous chapter, introducing the opposite emotion is a quick fix to emotional excesses. It is the art of overriding your current feelings with something that directly contrasts it. It does not work for anxiety alone. It works for anger, impatience, sadness, and every negative feeling, and let's say it works for the positive ones too. But why should you use write off positive feelings for negative feelings? The only positive attitude you might want to write off is lust or sexual desires, particularly when you are around people you should not have sexual relations with.

There are three ways to introduce an opposite emotion automatically. That is, your mind declares for the different feeling the moment the first feeling comes into your mind. Here they are:

The three ways to introduce an opposite emotion into your mind

a. The use of a mantra and self-counseling

Introducing the opposite emotion requires a subconscious effort. It requires your mind to be able to present the feeling itself because it is hard for you to interrupt the flow of emotions in your soul. You will have noticed how hard it is for you to stop loving someone or stop being angry on your own. It is only effortless if your subconscious mind has already decided that you shouldn't get mad. That is when you hear voices in your head, like "Cool Mike, easy. Easy. You are a champion; you don't need this anger. You are a peacemaker. You are not going to ruin it with anger."

So, a mantra might help a lot in this regard. You should start by introducing some preset mantra into your mind. Specific mantras are used for health and religious reasons. You don't need those. You could sit and think of a simple phrase that your mind can effortlessly remember. One of my best friends, Matilda, fell in love with her husband's brother. She lost her breath and felt very anxious every time she was around him, and she felt ashamed about it. She didn't want to break up her marriage, but she was going wild for him every passing day. She had to control herself urgently! "I am not going to love Selina," she started drumming into her head. She would tell it to herself every second, every minute, and everywhere she found herself.

Eventually, this mantra stuck to her mind so firmly that it manifested each time she saw her husband's brother. It would drum in her head and take over her spirits. Till she eventually accepted that there is no loving Selina. She was sticking to her husband. Counseling yourself and using a mantra can handle any kind of emotion, even love! So, before your wild emotions turn you to prey for psychological hecklers, heal yourself!

b. **Arts**

Arts is another fantastic way to heal yourself from any emotional distress. As empirical research has revealed, humans are always appealed to by one art or another. If you do not fancy music, then you probably love still or moving pictures. Other maybe you love paints, greenery, landscapes, oceans, skiing, diving, surfing. There has to be something you love!

I have no idea what you desire, but the solution you are looking for is sitting right there. If it is music, then you could turn to a lot of it when your emotions are going haywire. If it is painting, just get into your store and dig out your favorites. If going for a walk, skiing, or doing something different might help you change your mood, turn to it!

One last thing — dramas and comedies have been the world's panacea in recent years. All you need to change an emotion is to connect with the right medium that works for you. It reminds me of another friend who has a song that he listens to when he needs motivation. He has another when he feels he is not up to something, and he wants to roar his spirits to life. The long and short of this is that there is a cure in art. Check it out!

c. Physical and psychological relocation

Physical and psychological relocation is not entirely different from what we've talked about previously. Physical relocation refers to a deliberate change in your physical location. That is, you can change where you are at the moment, mainly if it is contributing to the emotions you feel. If you are getting too emotional about your dead uncle, for instance, you might try easing out of his home or away from the burial ground. If your fury is rising with your wife, it might be ideal to walk out of the house right away. You can fix jealousy, anger, and many other emotions that can be taken advantage of by psychic hecklers using this method.

Next to physical relocation is psychological relocation. If this is what you would be going for, you do not have to change your physical location at all. You simply have to shift your mind and shift your focus. If you were thinking about a dying friend, a lost job, or whatever makes you sad earlier, immediately changing your focus might make things a lot easier. Think about something else immediately, particularly a scene that makes you happy. It might be your little girl, the expression on your boss's face when she admits you are a great guy, or anything that makes you smile! Applying any of these can help you overcome emotional distress. Don't you agree? I bet you can see it. You just cannot be a subject of Dark Psychology by the end of this piece!

Tips to remember

You can control your emotions by adopting these methods:

1. Doing the mental math
2. Hitting the self-control button
3. Search for the opposite emotion

CHAPTER 5
DO YOU KNOW THE WEIGHT OF WORDS AND THE ACTUAL CAUSE OF YOUR ANXIETY?

First things first, let's wrap up our talks on anxiety before considering a different ball game. All through the last few chapters, we kicked some facts in the air about anxiety. We plainly pointed out how it is our body's instinctive reaction to danger and how it might become a terrible problem if it goes into excess.

Apart from those, various hacks to anxiety and tweaks to emotions were considered all through the previous chapters. Only one thing is missing, and you are about to find out what it is in this chapter. It is impossible to put an end to a problem if you do not know what causes it for certain. You might solve that problem with some other methods, but there are no assurances that someday the issue will not appear again, unless you fix it from its origin.

Another thing, your heckler might still decide to root the source of your anxiety if you left some lines. If your college lecturer realizes that you were always anxious, disorganized, and jumbled whenever you have a lot of tasks, she might decide to choke you with class projects. She would choke you to the point that your only choice would be to show up in her office and ask for her help. To avert situations that would leave you prey, you must fix your anxiety entirely from its roots.

Now, what are the roots of anxiety, and what are the primary causes behind anxiety disorders?

1. Life experiences

Experience remains the best teacher, as the Germans often posit. It will help you realize some steps you should never take and some things that you've done wrong. If you have got some experience with something, you can tell when it is heading south, and that is enough to make you breathe rapidly or have an increased heart rate — anxiety.

The foremost reason that you feel anxious about something is the experience you have had around it. If you have always known that everyone who tries it will fail, you will likely be scared when you choose to try it. If you have often failed when you handle too many things at the same time, you will typically find yourself sweating when you have a lot of assignments on your table at work. You will get a lump in your stomach, and you will become restless both physically and mentally. During times when you have no experience, you could be worried about how you will handle something since you've never done it in your life.

All of these imply that a lack of experience can make you tremble in your shoes when you set out to handle a new problem. Nevertheless, the experience itself should be considered a source of inspiration. You should never define the present by the future, and neither should you become overconfident about how you performed in the past.

2. Health factors

More often than not, people have several health problems that can be linked to anxiety. These health ailments make them quiver at the slightest note of anything that could scare or make them uncomfortable. Hypertension, depression, stress, and the trauma of a shock or saddening situation are handy examples of such. Diabetes, heart disease, and various respiratory ailments are possible health complications that may trigger anxiety too. However, you should get urgent medical attention if you have one of these underlying health issues, and you suspect it might be linked to your anxiety. If you don't know for certain, you might travel down your own history to see how you have fared. Were you the confident guy who never seemed to be afraid of anything prior to this health snag?

3. Traits

Traits is another possible medium through which people develop anxiety disorders. By default, some people have an extremely anxious personality types, and they can pass it to their children. But it's not just their children; it could be passed to nieces, nephews, cousins, or extended relations in general. If you notice that none of your parents seem overly anxious about anything and that is just not the way you are, you might want to check your extended family for someone with similar traits to yours.

Usually, this type of anxiety is linked to a particular thing. You might be particularly nervous and uneasy about talking to a crowd because that was the exact problem someone else had in the family. If this was the case, you can only manage it through a series of hacks recommended in the previous chapters. There are no assurances that you will be completely rid of anxiety towards this particular thing.

Now that anxiety is done and over with, do you know one other thing that gives you a way to your psychological hecklers? It is the words you utter. It makes you vulnerable in a way that you cannot imagine. Do you know the weight of your words? Do they often express your anxiety, your personality, your beliefs, and who you are? Do they trigger a strong motivation both inside and outside of you?

The weight of your words

In the words of Brenan Manning, "In every encounter we either give life or drain it; there is no neutral exchange." What this implies is that each time you tear your lips apart to voice something, you are either giving life or draining it. There is no neutral exchange.

Whether you intend or not, someone will become inspired or demotivated from every single utterance you make even when they are not meant to motivate or bring negative energy to anyone. You should know that you can be affected too. The words you say to people get to you, and so do the words you utter to yourself. They make up your personality, they are relayed with your subconscious, and that is what makes up the way we think!

Jamaru Emoto was one of the world's scientists who dared to test the power of words on nonliving entities. He wanted to figure out if the words we speak can affect plants or objects that cannot hear humans. He tried with some rice in a jar, and some water in vials. Each of the objects was split into two. He spoke negative words to one or asked people to utter negative words straight at it.

In other words, he made people pass their negative energy to one at the same time they passed positive energy to the other. He was surprised to discover that at the end of the experiments, the objects that were riddled with negative energy ended up badly. They underperformed when compared with those that were riddled with positive energy.

This brought him to the conclusion that energy is continuously circulated in the world. It is not just among humans — even objects, animals, and weather conditions pick hints from our lives. If plants or water could be stunted merely because of what we say to them, how do we describe the words we say to ourselves or other people? Can you remember the number of times you have cursed yourself, your kids, or your staffers? What if you are directly contributing to their underperformance? You might think it is doing nothing to them or you really, but what if it is? You can verify Jamaru Emoto's research in a library. He might be proving a point that would change the rest of our lives if we adopt it. So, dare to test a different lifestyle.

Try to see how things would work for you, your friends, and colleagues if you radiate positive energy rather than negativity all through your lives. I should remind you that positivity reduces your anxiety. It is an excellent way to trim your emotional outbursts. And, subsequently, the activities of psychic hecklers in your life.

How can you practice positivity with your words?

a. Mind your thoughts

A famous philosopher once warned that you should "mind your thoughts because they become your actions." It is hardly possible for anyone to have rogue ideas in their mind and hide it for long. No matter how good you are, you will soon exhibit the thoughts in your mind somewhere. If you think life is harsh, ruthless, and everyone should be treated that way because that was how you were raised, you will likely reflect it in your behaviors.

You will find it difficult to help anyone in difficulty. If you think life is beautiful and straightforward despite all of what you have gone through, you will likely be easy on people. So, what you think is essential to how you act. Shift your thinking! Mantras and self-talks are the most effective means to achieve that. *You are not what or who you think you are; you are what you think!*

b. Try to worry about others

You have probably had reasons to slam other people because you didn't put yourself in their shoes. You saw things as their judge, rather than someone who has an idea of what they might be going through; you will likely have a different judgment of them when you try to understand. This is why every leadership training emphasizes empathy. If you want to watch the words you spill more, simply try to be empathetic!

c. No name-calling!

Empathy or no empathy, there should be no name-calling for anyone! You have to cultivate it from this moment. You should no longer tell yourself, "I am so stupid, I am such an idiot, I am such a klutz," et cetera. No name calling! And as much as you will be stopping it for yourself, it has to be stopped for everyone too — not even the politicians or the cops. No name calling for anyone. This is going to be super hard, but if you try it and it doesn't change your life, write to me!

d. Be happy and positive

Positivity is the habit of conditioning your mind in a manner that it stays full of hope and happiness, regardless of what you are fighting on your own. No one might notice how much you are putting up with, but you should never be bothered. Staying positive can reflect in your entire lifestyle, your habits, and your conditions. If you try to be happy, you will likely not be pressed or frustrated by what people say or do. Instead, you will be able to control your emotions effortlessly.

e. Change your circle

Your circle refers to the people around you. It refers to the type of people who make up your world. Are they friends who make you get upset all the time? Are they people who do not believe in patience and peace? Are they people who frustrate you to the point you often have to slam or curse them? It is way better to let them go than continue to curse everyone. Check your environment, anything that erupts negative energy should leave!

f. Shut your eyes to it

What were they doing wrong this time, and would it please you to look away once in a while? You can control your words better if you learn to look over several things that you consider a little bit improper. The first fact is that no situation can be perfect for you to a tee. That is why you are a human; you are not structured to be satisfied. If you have to complain each time you are not satisfied, you will do it all the time. There is hardly a way you will complain all the time, and you will be free of negative words. To avoid radiating negative energy, look over many things!

Tips to remember

1. Your words are weighty!
2. You need to be positive!

THE OTHER

CHAPTER 6
DARK PSYCHOLOGISTS? THEY ARE LYING TO YOU

All through the last five chapters, we have extensively talked about SELF. I have shown you several ways that you may be vulnerable to manipulative vultures in human skin. Now, who are these Dark Psychology vultures? How do they operate? What is Dark Psychology? This is what we will extensively discuss in the next five chapters. Starting with this chapter, let's find an answer to one burning question:

What is so bad about Dark Psychology if no one is talking about?

Manipulation is one of the most popular interests in psychology. As I pointed out earlier, you will find millions of books about it in modern libraries all over the world. These books tell stories of how kings and heroes have fallen to cunning manipulation. They record different tales of how people learn the arts of exploitation.

This is precisely what Dark Psychology is doing to the world today. It poses as a remedy to your lifelong dreams to own power and rule the world. In reality, everything you have ever heard about this psychology is inhuman. It is far from human nature and they are lying to you. You will live the rest of your life as a human exploiter if you dare to believe.

Humans are expected to be unassuming, good-natured, democratic, and fair to everyone in the world. If you practice belief in the exploitation of others, you are everything different from all of the people in your world. It is time we call off the buff of Dark Psychology and wipe it off with what the world deserves. Before I tell you what the world deserves, let me fix this from the root.

What exactly is Dark Psychology?

In the exact words of Michael Nuccitelli, "Dark Psychology is both a human consciousness construct and study of the human condition as it relates to the psychological nature of people to prey upon others motivated by psychopathic, deviant or psychopathological criminal drives that lack purpose and general assumptions of instinctual drives, evolutionary biology, and social sciences theory."

I apologize if you don't like long definitions, and I agree that Michael Nuccitelli did go a little bit far. Nevertheless, he pointed out everything we ever need to note about Dark Psychology. It is the tendency of people to prey upon others (people, animals, or objects) due to their psychopathic or criminal drives. He believes that theories in evolutionary biology and social sciences might have discovered a lot about the psychology of human exploitation.

The crucial point is that it is the tendency of people to prey upon other people's minds due to their criminal or personal drives. Where Rachel Harris and every Dark psychologist is getting it wrong is unmistakable. She said Dark Psychology could help one to get better by learning about subtle persuasion, manipulation, and mind control. How can anyone get better in life when they have a criminal or psychopathic drive and prey on other people's minds? Something is not connecting. They are lying to us.

If you desire to get better in life and learn the subtle art of persuasion, manipulation need not be included in your lessons. Michael Pace, a learned psychologist, gives a note on manipulation: *"It is a common misunderstanding that influence and manipulation are the same things. This is not the case. Manipulation refers to the underhand and hidden process of influence that takes place outside the awareness of the person being controlled. The intention behind influencing someone as opposed to the intention behind manipulating them is another key difference."*

You do not have to exploit the mind of anyone or victimize other creatures. Even when they pose as if they are out to help you, there is always psychopathic drive behind this help. It is just as Michael Pace says, *"An influencer has the mindset of 'I would like to help you make decisions that are good for you.' A manipulator has the mentality of 'I want to control you to benefit myself secretly.'"*

Michael Nuccitelli pointed out that Dark Psychology is manifested in different ways. He notes that handy examples of its expounders are arsonists — people who take delight in burning houses, homes, and the resources of people. Nothing thrills them more than a setting a fire ablaze. Predators who try to hack into people's data on the internet is another example. They appear to be the friends of their victim on the internet as though they are the unsuspecting victim. You might earnestly try to provide an answer to my burning question: Is this the same kind of psychology that the world is dying to be built upon? Of course, they don't tell you these levels. They simply tell you it teaches you the art of persuasion, as well as manipulation, which ought to be replaced with "influence." It is glaring. They are lying to you.

The horrors of Dark Psychology.

1. **It champions manipulation**

Manipulation, is the handling, controlling, or using of something or someone to get what you want. It is the deliberate act of exploiting others just so your desires can be achieved. This word doesn't exist in the definitions of Dark Psychology by a grievous error; it is indeed a component of human exploitation. The natural law of humanity points out that men should be equal, even when some step out to lead others.

Men are not equal in a scheme like this; some will be relegated for the rest of their lives. They will have to do the bidding of someone else.

They will live to fulfill someone else's dream and never realize theirs. In the manipulation projected by Dark Psychology, the victims do not achieve their life goals. Whatever they do is always tailored towards the dream of their manipulator. Just go back and think about the life of Ken, and think about your own life too. You will realize that, even at times, your psychic heckler made you feel like you were achieving what you wanted while you were actually working towards what they ultimately desired. Manipulation is a violation in White Psychology; we said it in the first chapter, and we will only expose more as we go deeper!

2. Exploitation of empathy

Empathy is the ability to feel, think, and imagine things the way another person experiences it. It is your ability to put yourself in someone else's shoes and understand precisely what they are going through. When you are empathetic, you do not only see through the pains, you can imagine yourself feeling them and the disheartening plunges like the person who was directly affected. Empathy helps you understand why a worker may underperform at work. It enables you to imagine what your daughter, husband, or colleague might be going through after a trauma in their life. Empathy is a crucial skill for you as a leader, a motivator, and a teammate.

As thrilling as empathy sounds, it is always exploited by the Dark psychologist. It is often used in a way that the unsuspecting victim is hacked through their emotions. As Dark psychologists observe, a psychic heckler tries to understand her victim's feelings. She tries to feel them as much as the victim, and she puts herself in the position of the partner. Then, she begins to penetrate her victims by pretending to provide solutions to the victim's pains. Do you remember the illustration I gave earlier?

Imagine you have spent all of your life with a woman, and she suddenly dumps you for someone else on the eve of your marriage. If a heckler were around, she would figure out that you are in terrible pain, and you would earnestly want to get one over your ex-lover. She might offer to track this lover down or get you someone else. It would seem like she was helping out when, in reality, she had always wished you didn't marry the woman who left you. You are not fulfilling your desires in this situation. You are meeting someone else's. This is something that would never happen with White Psychology. No one is alive to manipulate. We would rather try to fix our life snags for one another. That's what humans should do!

3. **It is an oppression of the weak**

If you have ever hated the oppression of the weak, this is it staring you in the eye! Dark

Psychology *is* the outright oppression of the weak. How else shall we describe a situation when you wait till someone needs something and exploit them through what they lack? As a chap, if you spend all of your life like this, you may not live long enough to enjoy the proceeds of your exploitation. For one, if you influence people to do things for you as though they are helping themselves, some of them might hunt you down after they figure out that you have used them.

Besides that, you could live miserable for the rest of your life. When everyone else is impacting lives, growing as humans, and assisting the weak, you are doing just the opposite. At the end of the day, people will typically realize that you have been using them, and they will bring you down at all costs, even if they have to pay with their life. You will have no one to help you in your trying times. You will find it difficult to trust anyone. All because you chose to exploit someone when you could help them. Is it really worth so much?

4. Deceit is the game

The whole philosophy of White Psychology is built against deceit, exploitation, unfairness, and bias. If you ever need to describe the entire system of exploiting someone else to get your desires, you will agree that it is based on deception. You are deliberately trying to trick someone into doing your bidding. You are fooling them in a setup that seems like you are trying to support them. Even if you were ever going to lead people places, it is never done by tricking them. Dark Psychology goes against the code of humanity!

5. No freedom for humanity

Whatever holds you down does not offer you freedom. If someone tries to deceive you, manipulate you, and exploit you — all so that they can control you — they are not here to offer you freedom. They are not putting you in physical chains. It is mental and psychological chains that will alter your thinking forever. Do you have a friend who grew up the same way you did, only to change to a religious sect at some point? Perhaps they became a Jehovah's Witness, a Salafi Muslim, or any of the other powerful sects you can think of. You will realize that they choose to bond themselves in a completely different mindset. They live, think, and act according to their doctrines. That is not freedom, but they want it, and that is fine. In the case of psychic heckler's victims, they didn't choose to live that way. Their heart was pierced and penetrated when they were not looking!

Dark Psychology implies that you will be holding someone under your claws, or that the manipulation of someone else will catch you. It is not a "live and let live" situation. You either fight or perish, and that is more animalistic than humane. You can handle problems on your own. You can grow, become independent, and be free of narcissist clings. This is particularly important for you as a youth. You have your dreams, your desires, and you must not let them under what someone thinks you should do. If you want a thrilling life, you can learn to influence. You never have to manipulate. Steer clear of Dark psychics!

Tips to remember

1. Dark Psychology is a cruel joke on humanity.

2. Dark Psychology stands for everything wrong about human relations.

3. You need a better system!

CHAPTER 7
THE HECKLER AND THEIR PSYCHOLOGICAL PROFILING

Now that we have extensively dealt with the concept of Dark Psychology, we might as well discuss the psychics themselves. Who are these psychics? What do they want from you?

The first shock about these questions is that hecklers are not aliens. They are raw, natural, casual, human beings like you and I. Another stunning reality is that they are not a race that populate the next continent or lived in the past. They are here, in your world, in your life, and your relations. They are people you meet every single day of your life. I cannot tell for sure if your marital partner or parent is a heckler.

But I can assure you that hecklers, more often than not, appear as your brothers, sisters, parents, relatives in general, colleagues, friends, and everyone who has a seat in your life. What makes them psychic hecklers is their mindset. It is the goal with which they relate to other people, particularly you. If you choose to identify hecklers, you will likely head nowhere by finding where they live or how they look. They are practically everywhere. What you should find instead is the psychological profiling of hecklers.

Psychological profiling, now what's that?

As documented by the department of Forensic psychology in the United States, psychological profiling is the process of linking an offender's actions at the crime scene with their most likely characteristics to help the police investigators narrow down and prioritize a pool of most likely suspects. In other words, it is an attempt to find a criminal by picking out their distinguishing characteristics. The police initiated it, but psychologists are often invited to handle this part.

Now, what has that got to do with you?

Let me show you. A person who seeks to subjugate you, quell your dreams, and put out your creative ability is a criminal. The earlier you begin to see them that way, the quicker you find your way out of their path. I did say that they are among the people you come by in your everyday life — that is not very different from unidentified criminals. You come across them all the time, you just didn't know they were a serial killer; that everyone should flee from them the instant they appear. The police don't know either. The only way they can figure out who a criminal is is by the traits that they are trying to tail through psychological profiling. Now, as it is your responsibility to guarantee your safety and security, you must also carry out psychological profiling. It will help you to identify the people who have been hecklers in your life, as well as those who are tactically taming you to become their prey.

Great! So, what are the components of a psychic heckler's psychological profile?

1. They are narcissists!

What was that lesson you learned about narcissists? Frankly, even if you know close to nothing, you know that narcists are egocentric individuals who want nothing other than what pleases them. They care for nothing except what appeals to them and whatever edges towards satisfying their hearts' desires. Narcissists are humans like every other person — they are just more self-centered than you would expect of an average human being. If a person has such traits, there is every possibility that they will attempt to manipulate others to get what they desire. The next time you critically review the people at your workplace, sports arena, family, and circle in general, a narcissist is something you should look out for. If you find anyone with those traits, you may want to analyze your relationship with that person. There is every tendency that they have exploited you to get what they desired at some point. If they haven't done it with you, they probably did it elsewhere. You only need to listen more to people's comments about them, and you will find your answers.

2. They are tricksters!

Another tricky fact — more than half of the tricksters around you are manipulators. Tricksters are people who pull a fast one on you just to have fun. They are people who play pranks, jokes, and tricks either to entertain themselves or other people around them. While many of them may stay within limits, a large number of tricksters often step beyond the necessary. They might go past casual fun to the point of tricking you to believing things or making you the subject of their tricks. If you hate being made fun of, you might have problems with these trickers. But that is not even the weightiest problem; the issue begins when they sell you on absurd things.

They can sugarcoat lies in a way that your head would spin when they present it. You could be lured to believe they have just offered you an opportunity, or they were telling nothing but the truth. Often, it turns out that it was just a prank! This usually happens with someone like your sister who likes to trick you into believing lies. You are certainly going to find out in the end, and they will declare that it was a joke. Now, that's fine.

However, if anyone is still pulling jokes on you in your 20s and they are always convincing when they pitch it, you should never put your trust in them. They are hecklers. As much as I hope your lover and friends do not fall into this range, they likely do. If your friend or partner seems smart at tricking people and you, who knows them pretty well, also falls for their jokes, I insist that your partner is a heckler and you want to mind your relations with them.

3. They want you to do their bidding

Is there someone around you who always wants everyone else to do their bidding? That may be another clue you need to identify the psychic heckler in your circle. Humans are insatiable by default. Your parents, boss, and superiors will naturally request for some support and they will want you to follow some of their commands. You can differentiate someone who needs some tasks done from someone who wants to win at all times.

No matter how we try, we can't always get what we want. In cases where we clash with other people over certain things, we must understand as adults that we cannot always win. If you have someone who does not believe that they have to lose sometimes, you might want to reserve yourself from that person a little bit. In particular, if this person is well in their 20s or higher and they do not believe that they could lose.

4. They don't think you can both win

Why should you win at all when they can do all the winning? Shouldn't the winner be clear from the loser? That is the exact type of thinking that a heckler adopts. They are egocentric, power-drunk, intent on reserving power, and the "let and let live" mindset just doesn't work for them. The fascinating thing about such people is that they are not necessarily the most deserving of victory — they often underperform to the point that they do not deserve to be considered the winner.

They are often eager to be the leader, and as you might have guessed, it is for subjugation, manipulation, and exploitation. If someone has exhibited these features in your circle, they have probably given you everything you need to understand the kind of person that they are. There is a chance that they have deceived you or someone around just to get what they want.

5. Hypnotism is their weapon

Would you like to know the biggest manipulator in your circle? It is the storyteller. It is the person who convincingly presents facts that would be impossible to protest, refuse. Every brilliant lawyer in the world falls into this pit. No surprises, lawyers are the biggest manipulators in the world. They often have to twist facts with fiction to suit their illustrations in court.

We can understand the situation of lawyers. If there are people around you who can weave facts and fiction into an intricate presentation, you should be careful of them. Do you remember that friend who never loses an argument among your friends? That's them. That's the person you should be cautious of regarding their demands and how you respond. An awkward fact is that such hecklers are often more outspoken than most other people you have met in your life. They are tactical, logical, and enjoyable to listen to, and that is precisely why worming into people's hearts is a piece of cake to them.

6. They are overly empathetic

An empathetic person is sympathetic. He understands the words you are not willing to say; he can complete your sentences for you when you try to explain in distress; he sees people all too clearly. In fact, an empathetic person tends to understand you more than anyone else in the world. They are often so attentive and close to the point that they are the first person you want to talk to when you run into distress or are anxious about something.

This is awkward. Your friends and family are the only people who understand you better, with your parents and partner falling into this category more than anyone else. Does that mean that they are psychic hecklers too? Not exactly. They may not necessarily seek to rule your heart and compel you to do things for them. But yes, they are in the position to manipulate you. A person who you listen to in your time of distress can work their way to instill their ideas in your mind while you are seeking them out. So, they are in an excellent position to exploit you. There is no running from such people. It is no different from trying to escape criminals to a place where there are no criminals — as long as you are on earth, that is practically impossible as criminals are everywhere. You only have to be conscious of how you relate with them, now that you have an idea of how they can be harmful to you. You should not swallow every recommendation hook, line, and sinker. Critically think about everything!

7. **They are nosy**!

This is an easy one. There are people around you who want to have an idea of everything that is happening in the world. Despite the long fence between you and your neighbors, some of them still crane their necks to pick out the tiniest noise in the other house. A person who spreads rumors here and there cannot exactly be good luck. They could have some manipulative news that would be hard to refute because you know that they often get information.

People like these come into your life to tell you that your girlfriend is sleeping with someone else, your boss isn't planning to promote you, everyone is talking thrash about you, and all the bad news you can imagine. They are manipulative too. So, you want to be extra cautious of how you relate to them.

8. Manipulators

It is essential to point this out despite that you might have guessed it already. Psychic hecklers are the biggest manipulators around you. Even when something looks blue to everyone on Earth, they could argue that it is green and would come bearing proof. Regardless of whether they do it with pleasure or pressure, they have given hints and insights into how they could manipulate things if it becomes necessary. You do not have to avoid these people, since your parents, friends, and even a life partner may fall into these categories. You only have to ensure that you do not let your guard down at anything lest you become their puppet.

9. Aggression and exploitation

To bring things to a close, I should tell you that aggression is a prominent feature of a manipulator. Several times, they realize that they are losing grip of a situation, and they try to gain it back with aggression. They expect total submission to their demands and do not necessarily have more wealth or power than everyone else. They are just aggressive and violent. People like these are glaring hecklers. Avoid them if you can!

As a reminder, humans have different personalities; some people may appear aggressive naturally without having the mind to manipulate. Even you might have one of these manipulator traits without having a desire to manipulate anyone. This gives a clue that there are different personalities, and it is essential to distinguish a natural behavior from a manipulator's façade. To make this doubly clear, we will consider the different characters of humans in chapter 11.

Tips to remember

1. A psychic heckler is a real individual.
2. A psychic heckler tries to penetrate and manipulate you.
3. The psychic heckler has some unmistakable features — you can scent one a mile away.

CHAPTER 8
HOW TO NOT BE MANIPULATED

As you can see, these people are super close to you. They are people you have to interact within your daily lives. Some of them are close to the point that cutting them off would mean that you are shutting yourself from extremely crucial people. They are your friends, your dad, your mom, husband, or even child. So, how does anyone cut people like that out of their life?

The good news is that, rather than cut things off with these people, there are convincing ways you can ensure no one ever manipulates you. There are simple steps and points to remember each time you deal with these people. As long as you put them into practice, you will live your life without budging to these people.

So, what are the ways you can avoid manipulation?

a. Be conscious

Unlike the general definition of consciousness, consciousness here implies that you are alert and on your toes while you are awake. It is a deliberate effort to catch a glimpse of every activity going on around you. Being conscious implies that you do not only receive and respond to signals in your environment; you are equally able to interpret and decode this signal. It means that you clearly understand what is going in your world, and you can actively take part. This is not the end — you can also recognize unclear signs that no one is talking about.

Let's get practical: You need to keep your guards up at all times. Manipulators are looking to penetrate you when you are not looking. They are looking to exploit you just when you assume that you are having the thrill of the moment. Your manipulator might sound very amusing, inspiring, or emotional. It could get so high that you forget they can get into you with their acts, and you let down your guard. You do not know who is aiming to tweak your mind so you can achieve their wills. So, you must never let down your guard at any point.

b. Analyze and validate

Validation is an essential feature of quality information. It is the extra effort you apply to ensure that a piece of information is spot on. It should not matter whether you are listening to a politician, a classroom teacher, or a priest — you need to always verify whatever people say to you.

It is one way you will never be swayed off your feet by fantabulous fallacies. You will also be able to tell who is telling the truth from whoever is there just to deceive you.

The moment you identify deceit and its proponents, you should know that manipulation is in the making. Whoever sits and thinks of lying to you is swaying you from the truth. They are trying to make sure you do not see the reality or believe in it. Whether for personal, political, or communal gain, whoever refuses to state the facts is a manipulator. Avoid them. One easy way to get to know them is to analyze and validate whatever facts you receive from them.

c. Know your fundamental rights

Your fundamentals rights are, as you know, the rights you should be accorded irrespective of the circumstances. They are the basic rights that everyone should have as long as they are human. These rights are often trampled upon by psychic hecklers. You will need to hold onto them when you meet hecklers who try to blackball your liberty. In particular, aggressive hecklers often press down people's rights, and they hardly ever tolerate opposition. They defiantly try to suppress you from challenging their authority. As long as you do not harm anyone in any way, you can stand your ground and ensure your fundamental rights that pertain to your health are not hampered.

These are the possible rights that may be infringed by psychological hecklers:

• The right to expression of wants, feelings, and opinions.

• The right to fair business; that you should be served when you pay. People should be offered quality when they pay for it.

• The right against physical or psychological manipulation.

• The right to make priorities.

• The right to health and happiness

• The right to make solid "No!" and "Yes!" decisions without fear or interference from anyone.

d. Avoid those that you can

Avoiding people implies that you try to escape their presence as much as possible. It is you trying to steer clear of people because they possess strong traits of a psychic heckler. This will be stupidly easy if your identified heckler is a distant colleague, an acquaintance, or someone who doesn't mean much in your life. If the person is as close as a relative or sibling, it might get a little more tricky, though it is entirely possible. You only have to ease yourself out as soon as possible when they sit around. Think of a valid excuse and escape their sight as much as possible. Let someone else pick up the phone and do the talking when they call.

Avoiding people is an effective way to duck any harms from them. If they don't see you often, you will less likely be a subject in their thoughts. Even if you were earlier, they think about you less when they do not see you and they will likely focus on much easier prey soon. If this were your lover, parent, or someone super close, it might be tough to avoid them. But you have to try your best, since chronic manipulators can hardly change their lifestyle. You should try to change, but you should not dwell on it. If they would change, a little hint from you is enough.

e. Engage them and stand your ground

Engaging manipulators is another way to increase your chances of not being manipulated. As empirical studies have revealed, psychic hecklers often attack your spirit when they realize that they have the upper hand. You have fallen for their emotional façade, and you are offering little or no resistance. This is why you must not let that happen. Do not be swayed by the flowing spirit of a psychic heckler. If your dad is getting angry and the atmosphere seems tense in a manner that everyone else would cower and give in to his demands, do not! If your mom is getting so emotional that every other child would have dropped their desire to join the arms and hold force, you should not! I have pointed out the series of emotions you can expect from a heckler in the previous chapter.

Rather than be swept off by their display, engage them. Ask them questions about what they are asking of you. "Does this look appealing to you? Will I have a say in this? What do you stand to gain from this?" Ask them questions that might throw them off balance. Many exploiters are scared; they merely wear a façade and appear aggressive. Facing them head-on might help you break that bogus confidence.

f. Give a diplomatic NO

"How to give a diplomatic NO" is something you should learn. You must be able to reject propositions of manipulators without appearing aggressive. Being diplomatic implies that you are objective, cautious, and you hold a firm ground, and you are not aggressive in its defense. Anyone who wants to manipulate will know a lot of things about you. They might have thought you will be easy prey since you are always compliant. Your most important mission in that moment is to say NO and hold on to it, without sounding weak or aggressive.

If you are also the explosive type, they probably have an idea of how you will react. They knew you would explode, and the ambiance will go up in flames pretty soon. They will be able to exploit that and make it work to that advantage. Now, you have to be different too. You have to give a resounding 'no' without sounding overboard. A diplomatic NO is formal, stable, and enough to pass your point across.

g. Try to buy time

Psychic hecklers have always known one thing: If people had enough time, they would think things through and change their minds about everything. So, they try to make sure that their victims never get that time to think. What do they do then? They present their case in an urgent manner and you are compelled to take action almost immediately. They try to pressure you to see some urgency. Have you noticed it at all? You might want to pay attention the next time you run into a psychic heckler. That is their weapon!

And that is precisely what you will take from them. You should never be pressured to make decisions in a hurry. No matter how urgent a situation seems, you need time. You have to ALWAYS think things through before settling on something.

h. Avoid taking the blame

There is no reason you should ever take the blame for psychological hecklers. They were the assailants; it is no use blaming yourself for being attacked. Rather than spend all of your time lamenting, brace yourself to get better for the next time.

i. Never be the subject of talk

There is an extremely high chance that you will be talked about when you are the subject of discussion. But it doesn't end there. It is a convenient avenue for people to see through you and realize your weaknesses. Anyone who will attack your mind to win it will first have to recognize your shortcomings. Even if you do not go about talking about your weaknesses, they can be effortlessly deduced from what everyone is saying about you while you sit. You do not want to expose yourself. So, avoid being the subject of talk. Concurrently, you should not discuss others if you do not fancy being discussed.

Apart from that, a psychic heckler will be triggered to think about you more when they hear or talk more about you. Instead, try this if you are speaking with one of them: "Hey, Fred. How was work today? Did you break the ice with your boss?"

"Sure. I did. You tell me, did you turn up at work at all...?"

Turn the subject to them, and not you!

One other thing you should never forget is self-confidence. Anyone trying to work their way into your heart is not so different from you. They are just another person with a lot of guts and confidence. They think the walls of their heart are secure, and now they can attack another person's heart. Show them the mistake in their thinking and strictly remember that you are not going to manipulate them in turn. Reason things out and defend yourself!

Action Plans

1. Do not be manipulated!
2. You have got rights, explore them!
3. Give a diplomatic NO

4. Try to buy time
5. Avoid those that you can

CHAPTER 9
THE BRIDGE BETWEEN ANXIETY AND ANGER

By now, you clearly understand that anxiety is a nervous feeling that you are unable to get out of your body. It outlines every feature of discomfort, uncertainty, and all forms of negativity. Being anxious implies that you fail to understand your body system, that you realize something is amiss and are unable to hold the right end of the stick.

Anger is a little bit different. It is a furious downpour of emotion that exerts excess energy. When you are fiercely angry about something, you are ready to fight to the last breath for or against it, depending on your perspective. An anxious person would be unwilling to fight, no doubt. Still, there is a delicate connection between anger and anxiety —a gentle bridge that you have always missed because of its flakey nature.

Before our discussion on this connection, let's brush on some pertinent facts. Anxiety can affect you in two ways, and they are your emotions and your health. When you are anxious, you will likely experience several abnormalities in your health. Some of them are: the rapid increase in your pulse or heartbeat, headache, the release of excitement hormones, restlessness, sleeplessness, and so on. At the emotional level, several changes happen too. These changes have longer lasting effects on you than your health conditions. Some of the emotions are fear, impatience, psychological imbalance, and distraction. The worst of these feelings is anger. Anger? Yes. This brings us to the connection between anger and anxiety.

The bridge between anger and anxiety

Anger is one of the top damaging influences of anxiety. It is a psychological imbalance that results from getting curious and uncomfortable about something. When you get overly concerned and anxious about a situation, you will likely begin to think about it at all times. You will find little peace until you are able to find a way around it. Your restlessness may result in a wave of anger that you cannot explain. It can turn you into a furious and tireless person who will not rest until you find the solution. It may also turn you into an aggressive person out of fear and insecurity.

Simply put, anxiety may have no way out until you get angry about it and restlessly reach out for an answer.

From an entirely different perspective, anxiety may also trigger aggression in you. You may become so anxious, nervous, and uncomfortable that you begin to get aggressive to everyone who comes around. This aggression will have generated from that bottled up anger and anxiety that has been created in you.

In an intricate network, anger and anxiety are connected beyond this explanation. They are connected in the soul much more than you expect. And there is hardly a better way to describe this than Plato's Tripartite theory. The Tripartite theory? Yes, Plato was the brain behind that. He was the first person who believed that the human soul could be partitioned into three distinctive entities:

a. The Logistikon
b. The Thymoides
c. The Epithymetikon

These three entities are believed to be in control of our respective lives. Each one of them is responsible for a distinct form of our feelings or behavior, and they work together to form a complete structure. Plato also explains that the three entities grow differently. Your nature and that of every other human being are determined by which of these entities develop more. Let's explain their functioning.

a. The Logisitikon

According to Plato, the Logistikon is just the way it sounds — it is the part of the human soul that coordinates logic. It shapes up a person's chain of reasoning and the pace at which they can apply logic to situations. Plato suggests that leaders, philosophers, and people who have a need for sharp thinking and sound judgment use it. If a person's logisitikon develops much more than the other parts, he would likely think more; he will be more critical than emotional. He will tilt towards evaluative and judgmental reasoning. This is something we must always understand about people. If they are unbending with rules, they probably developed Logisitikon much more than the two others.

b. The Thymoide

The Thymoide is another feature of the human soul as perceived by Plato. It is the flip side of the Logistikon. It does not emphasize creative thinking or emphatic reasoning; instead, it emphasizes emotional development. It sits that your feelings and instincts are the most important weapons you need as a human. This is why a person who develops Thymoide more than every other one would be more emotional than realistic. They would rather appeal to what they feel than the facts available to them. If that is you, you will realize that you are often more anxious than other people.

c. The Epithymetikon

The Epithymetikon is not in league with the two others at all; it is a whole different ball game. It emphasizes that there is another section of the Tripartition that lays on desires rather than thinking or feelings. According to Plato, this part of the human brain pays attention to our longings and aspirations. It is the part that triggers anger over what you aspire and cannot acquire.

Each of parts of a functioning soul is relatively different. Nevertheless, they need to work together to ensure that you have a balanced life. So, you must find a way to make them work together. None of them is missing in every human. You only need to pay some more attention when you figure out that one pronounced than the others. For instance, if you are always anxious about everything, your Thymoide may be more developed than the others. At the very least, you need to improve your Logistikon and Epithymetikon. This will help you find a balance in life. It will help you bridge anxiety and anger, and it will help you control yourself before manipulators!

Tips To Remember

There is a sensitive bridge between your anxiety and anger. Find this gap!

THE PLACE

CHAPTER 10
DUMP EVERYTHING YOU KNOW ABOUT PSYCHOLOGY

Here and now, we will consider the last part of the revelation we have been unveiling. We have emphasized the SELF and the OTHER. Now, it is time to expansively discuss the PLACE. What is "the Place" about? Why does it matter? I am going to hold nothing back. Trust me.

First, you should recall that we have talked about two vital segments that will be connected at this point. I have shown you how you can remain resilient against all sorts of manipulations and psychic hecklers, and we have extensively discussed the concept of White Psychology. What is the link between the two, and how can you steady your feet on the path of White Psychology? That's what I will break down all through this chapter and to the conclusion of this book.

So, in this chapter, we will focus on one thing, dumping everything you have learned about Psychology. What were the fanciful fallacies you have heard about yourself? What was not right about your philosophies about life? Let me show you what you have never known about yourself through the relational identity.

The Relational Identity (R.I)

In the words of David Sluss and Ashforth, Relational Identity is the nature of one's role in a relationship and how this role influences one's attitude in each case. In manager to subordinate, parent to child, or coworker to coworker relationships, these relational identities are remarkably different. It is an attempt to explain that one's role or situation may determine how one relates to a given condition.

According to the R.I. philosophy, a human being should not be classified as a species with a constant identity. This is because her condition, her relationship level, and such similar factors may determine how she relates in each period. Let's consider a handy illustration: In the workplace, you would likely not associate with the manager of your company the way you would relate to coworkers and other staff members. Your relation with your wife would be somewhat different from how you'd associate with the kids. The only cause of these dynamics is that humans have relational identities.

All through modern psychology, it is always assumed that humans have a stable, predictable, and reliable personality. It is believed that once you appear harsh to a few people, you are always harsh, and you will never be kind. This is why it might surprise anyone if you soften a bit in your interactions with a few people. If you seem nice to everyone around you, you will be expected to be kind all through, too. Many people might be shocked if you go hard on anyone. This is one of the blatant errors in modern psychology that you have also kept in your mind. It is not valid. You feel reluctant to show a different behavior because you assume you must be found with only one attitude at all times. Have you ever asked yourself questions like these?

"How would it sound to everyone else if gentle Paul thrashed a boy who stole his ball?"

"How would it sound that ruthless Jack cried for a girl who lost her candy?"

If it is a yes, which it likely is, you feel that way because you have conditioned yourself to believe that you have only one fixed character, and you must be found with nothing else. What nobody told you was your relational identity. You are not a species with a fixed personality — the relation at hand prompts your character. Unmistakable proof of this is that a person would describe you as "kind, loving, hardworking, et cetera" and another person would instantly thumb you down, "that's not true, he is a brute!" The only explanation for this is that you have displayed different attitudes to each of them, according to the relations you had. Your identity is not static; it is only determined by the three factors we have emphasized from the start of the book. To put it straight, your identity is determined by "The Self, The Other, and The Place."

Do not forget: your identity is not only determined by your relationships. Several other factors come into play when you try to establish your identity. For example, your character may be influenced by your culture. You consider some specific ways of life as usual because it is the lifestyle adopted by your parents or those who raised you. You were given your name because it was considered normal in your culture. But your name is a mere label; if it was taken away, who would you be? It is time to forget the identity you have been given. It is a casual identity that ought not to be fixed in your psychology. You have been given your name, your culture, your style of life, and so much of your beliefs. If you are stripped of them, won't you still be someone?

You need to start seeing yourself beyond the limitations you have been put in all of your life. This is one guaranteed way you can wriggle out of exploitation, manipulation, and the wrenches of the psychic hecklers. When people realize that their philosophies do not condition your thinking and lifestyle, they give up trying to cow you. Henceforth, your sole objective should be to discover yourself. It should be to find out who you are and apply it in three basic operations.

1. Individual

The first reason you need to develop yourself is to recognize your individual identity. Your personality has always been shaped by the ideas passed by other people to you. You have built your unique character around uncertain identities. Finding your real identity helps you to know who you are.

2. Interpersonal

How do you relate to individuals in your world? You have been terribly wrong by attempting to connect with everyone the same way. You have to face the fact that different situations require different responses. There is no reason you should treat them the same way. If you can identify your personality and accept that you are not conditioned to act in a particular pattern, you can handle relationship crises better.

3. Collective levels

In general, your ability to discover yourself will influence your contribution to the community. It will affect your efforts, your growth, and your ability to solve problems in the community positively. The essence of development is that you cannot be useful to the world or anyone if you do not clearly understand yourself. To be clear, finding your relational identity is non-negotiable.

The perspective of reality

Now, it is all too clear that the perspective you see yourself is wrong. You have taken up these perspectives because your immediate community thrust them at you and made you hold them as your values. Nevertheless, you should know that the reality about you and your personality is hidden from how others perceive you, and how you see yourself. Let's not get fuzzy. — your reality is how others see you and how you make others think of you. As the Dalai Lama says, "If you can't change the world, change yourself." This is one reason we might touch on some common perspectives.

a. **Self**: The self refers to the stable and reliable image that you present to others. It is how you make others think of you. It describes how people will consider you on average, whether as intelligent, lazy, cautious, progressive, et cetera.

b. **Sense of Guilt**: In essence, your feelings of guilt borders around how you choose to see yourself. It refers to the perspective with which you consider yourself and your values. Several people assume that they are not valuable, that they do not deserve certain things in life, and that they should not even be given the opportunity. If you have always felt this way, your sense of guilt has been on the high side and you should seriously consider trimming it down. You have to consider stepping up your perspective about yourself. Your full features, abilities, and weaknesses should be figured out before you can successfully attempt to help anyone. It is as the saying insists: You are all at the center of your universe. Your ego-self-importance and self-realization are of no small importance. *"I am because we are"* —#Ubuntu

If you are still wondering how you can ever prioritize your ego, you can keep your eyes on the following. First, you should know that they are the relational functions that your egoistic instinct can help you to achieve. They are, as Darwin says, *competence without comprehension.* This summarily implies that they are actions that your body can perform with or without your knowledge. If you pay attention to these functions more, you stand a higher chance of knowing what you stand for.

The relational functions of the EGO

1. Thoughts

Thoughts refer to the simple flow of ideas in your mind. It covers your perspective on different issues and your intellectual contribution to the community. Your thoughts can determine your attitude to different situations and life in general. It determines your beliefs, your style of life, what you support, and what you counter. All of these determine how you spend all of your life. Hence, they can tell who you are to no small extent.

Think before you talk" is a maxim that must become valid for you from now on. You must begin to understand that you have to pay more attention to your words to develop your ego. You can change nothing if you do not change your mind, as Santosh Kalwar says, "We are addicted to our thoughts. We cannot change anything if we cannot change our thinking." In pertinent lines, Scottie Waves hints that, "If you realized just how powerful your thoughts are, you would never think a negative thought."

2. **Sensations**

A sensation is a signal sent by your body to your brain. It is a tingling that arises when your body receives some information and tries to process. Sensations come from what you perceive through your sense organs — what you touch, feel, see, hear, or smell. Your impression is one of the determining factors that prove who you really are. You might have no idea, but humans do not perceive things the same way. We may agree on certain general traits such as tasty, tall, pretty, ugly, et cetera.

On the critical approach, the sensation is always personal. You feel so strongly about something different from how everyone else feels about it. You might stare at objects and sense how they could turn out over time.

3. Sentiments

Your sentiments refers to your perspective or opinions that are held or expressed to the outer world. It refers to the perspectives and feelings that you hold over different situations. Your sentiments often arise from your thoughts and views of life. It is equally important to understand your sentiments when you seek to identify who you are. What do you think of your religion? What do you think about your passion, your job, your lifestyle? Your sentiments or feelings can help you figure out what you hold as personal philosophies.

Up to the present age, your sentiments are considered as important as feelings. This is what Honoré de Balzac implies by "But reason always cuts a poor figure beside sentiment, the one being essentially restricted, like everything positive, while the other is infinitive."

4. Intuition or instincts

Instincts refer to the guts feelings you have about something. It refers to the strong instinctive idea you hold onto even when there are no facts to bank upon. In many situations, your instincts contradict every fact available yet you hoose to use it to go by.

Instincts is one of the weirdest traits of a healthy human. You cannot hold it to the function of the human body, like sensation or thoughts. Yet, you hear your instincts as clear and distinctive as you can read the facts available. It gives a loud and unmistakable voice that has nothing to do with logic, research, or belief. By that, I imply that your instincts might contradict your beliefs. You might love the exact type of person you feel natural disgust for.

5. Morals

Your morals refers to your principles in a particular aspect of life; an umbrella that describes the standards and policies that you hold as right or wrong. It covers what you believe to be valid, acceptable, and unacceptable in the community. The troubling thing about morals is that they do not come from you. They are subconsciously imposed on you by the community where you grow. Many of these morals might make you feel uncomfortable, unsatisfied, and you might have some reservations for several of them.

6. Reason

Your reasoning is the translation of your perspectives on specific issues. It refers to the different angles with which you address pressing problems and how best you believe they can be solved. Your reasoning determines your contribution to talks, being among people, and community developments. Your reasoning determines how you approach situations, too.

As you pitch your place in life, the content of this chapter can be your compass. It can be your guide, and it can help you shape your personality. You only have to remember that you do not have a single character. You have a relational identity that is determined by the SELF, PLACE, and the OTHER.

Tips to Remember

1. Everything you held about yourself was wrong!

2. You are not a fixed entity, you are prompted to act by instincts.

3. You need to understand the concept of relational identity. That is how you know why and how you should relate!

CHAPTER 11
WHAT ARE THE EXPERTS
SAYING ABOUT YOUR ANXIETY?

What are the experts saying about anxiety?

In a practical sense, what do the scholars think about anxiety? Why does it matter to you? That's what I will tell you from this chapter to the conclusion. There are different perspectives on the actual cause of anxiety, and many scholars peg these causes to social and economic factors. However, there is a different perspective recommended by Jung and Gurdjieff. They believed that anxiety might be a natural feature of some human personalities. In essence, some human personalities tend to be more anxious than others. This brings us to wonder what the types of personalities are.

Jung recommended eight psychological types, and Gurdgeff believed that there are nine human personalities. They are considered the "Enneagram." Finding out where you belong, and recognizing the profile of your psychic heckler is a vital clue to escaping their claws. What are these personalities?

The nine personalities types by Gurdjieff

1. The Reformer

A Reformer is someone who has a strong sense of right and wrong. They are people with a keen sense of moral standards and ethics. They are naturally scared of making mistakes. These types of people tend to be a little bit anxious than others on average. Reformers appear like perfectionists. They want to experience a dramatic change in the community, and they throw caution into the wind. One striking thing about them is their distaste for criticism.

They earnestly hate to be condemned, and they are naturally impatient. If you have a personality like this, you would hate to be criticized. It might come as an advantage when your psychic heckler has this personality. They hate to be stained. So, standing up to them a few times might be enough to end the war. Plato, Osama Bin Laden, Bill Moyers, Martha Stewart, Sir Thomas More, Mahatma Gandhi, Michelle Obama, and Nelson Mandela are all members of this group.

2. The Helper

A Helper is precisely what he is called. He would be sincere, generous, and willing to step aside for people. He loves to contribute everything he can to ensure success and excellence. They are not usually possessive, and they put the needs of other people before theirs. If you are a Helper, you want to be needed, and you are always proud to be useful to other people. This is not bad in any way, since it makes you empathetic and helpful to other people.

However, you must understand that your tender heart makes you vulnerable to psychic hecklers. It takes little effort to exploit you and make you do things the way they desire; after all, you are willing to go out of your way by default. John Denver, Mary Kay Ash, Pope John XXIII, Richard Simons, Josh Groban, and many others are Helpers.

3. The Achiever

An Achiever is an attractive person who seems pretty lucky with life. She appears naturally charming. She is ambitious, and she has high aspirations. She spends a lot of effort chasing her dreams, and often, she achieves her desires. Achievers hate to be worthless, they are reasonably self-conscious. They are professional, and they revel in the thoughts of being valued, unlike a Helper who merely wants to be useful and not necessarily appreciated. There is a chance that you will come across Achievers everywhere, but the likelihood is higher at the workplace. Bill Clinton, Tony Blair, Truman Capote, Brooke Shields, and Elvis Presley are some of the people in this category. An Achiever tends to hack into other people's minds in a bid to manipulate them. Your best bet is to humbly step out of their way without attempting to undervalue them.

4. The Individualist

An Individualist is an unusually sensitive person. He is someone who understands his unique role in the universe. He recognizes himself as someone who deserves less attention from the world. Hence, he shies away at the slightest opportunities. If this were you, you might never agree to be vulnerable.

But something deep down has never stopped screaming that you are vulnerable to others in every way. An Individualist lives in melancholy and self-pity. He is honest, emotionally sensitive, and creative. He hardly finds beliefs that he has a strong personal significance that can be manifested. He spends a large part of his life finding himself. If this sounds a lot like your personality, you are easy to manipulate by anyone. This is particularly because you were always creating a space in your life for someone.

The instant a psychic heckler recognizes this vacuum, they try to penetrate through you and effortlessly win you over. Your best bet is to learn some self-worth and self-confidence. Do not settle for what someone says because it appears genuine. Stand up for yourself and be critical! Diane Arbus, Martha Graham, Jackie Kennedy, and Judy Garland are some people in this group that you might have heard about.

5. The Investigator

An Investigator is someone who appears naturally curious and attentive. He is intent, inventive, and he has complex ideas. He is alert, he has fast-thinking skills, and he is typically eccentric. An investigator does not care about having a team. They have a high goal that they chase on their own. They would likely not bow to oppression and pressure either. With a clear vision, they are competent, capable, and always willing to solve problems. The likes of Oliver Sacks, Agatha Christie, Emily Dickinson, Bill Gates, and Mark Zuckerberg are perfect examples in this category. People like these are tough to manipulate. If you are here, I'd better say congratulations.

6. The Loyalist

Being loyal and responsible is the number one feature of people in this category. They are typically reliable. They are hardworking, and they can spot trouble a mile away. They may not be straightforward, and they might get extremely nervous. They can be rebellious, too, particularly when they feel something is not right. They are cautious and slow to action, but they are also self-reliant. Overall, we can agree that they are a complicated type. They are courageous, independent, reliable, and can be counted upon. A loyalist is not easy to manipulate, and they are not easy to liberate. Mark Twain, Robert F. Kennedy, Malcolm X, Oliver Stone, and George Bush are all in this category.

7. The Enthusiast

The most prominent feature of an enthusiastic person is that she is an extrovert. She is always super excited, fun-loving, high spirited, scattered, and undisciplined. An enthusiastic person easily becomes distracted; they get bored easily, and they often look forward to new experiences happening soon. They try to focus on real goals, but the downside to this is that they often misapply their talents. They are versatile, but they hate being deprived. They hate getting moody, and they have an intense hatred for pain. Galileo Galilei, Thomas Jefferson, Leonard Bernstein, Malcolm Forbes, and so on belong to this class.

8. The Challenger

Challengers are the class of people with the highest tendency to be aggressive. They are naturally confident of themselves. They are assertive, bold, strong, and domineering. They want to lead at all times, and they do not take opposition from anyone lightly. They are protective by default, and they are resourceful. They hate being controlled by anyone, and they love being in charge of their destiny. They want to be celebrated, and they can be intimidating when they suspect that they are losing control. Temper will be one of your top problems if you belong to this category. Sometimes, your confidence can be inspiring, and a personality of this nature is tough to manipulate. On the flip side, having one around you means that you are at risk of manipulation. Donald Trump, Saddam Hussein, John Wayne, and Franklin D. Roosevelt are some of the famous people who fall into this category.

9. The Peacemaker

The last, but certainly not the least of Gurdgeff's Enneagram, are the Peacemakers. They are among the most reliable people, and they have a stable personality. You can tell the next thing they would do by studying them for a short while. They are creative with high standards, are typically supportive, and they appreciate a calm, serene world.

They try to keep peace with everyone around, though they can sometimes get reckless and lose control. They expect things to go smoothly and may not be fast at adjusting. They are scared of losing, and they can prove to be stubborn more than a mule. Am I describing you? Then you should know that you are prone to exploitation from people like the Challengers. You would likely step down effortlessly so peace could reign except for times that you clearly cannot cope. Queen Elizabeth II, Walt Disney, Carl Jung, and Joseph Campbell are some common examples.

Gurdjieff's Enneagram should have opened your eyes to who you are and how you fit into THE PLACE. It should have given you an insight into the types of people who fill your world and what you should expect from each person. This is not the end when it comes to finding out where you belong. Another perspective that can open your eyes to who you are in the Jung personality types.

The Jung Personality Types

In a bid to explain the different attitudes of humans, Jung suggested eight personality types, as I earlier mentioned. Before we put our heads together and table these types, I should let you know that Gurdgeff and Jung were not the only individuals who attempted to identify the varieties in personalities. There were several others, including Myers and Briggs. I have chosen Jung and Gurdgeff due to their pertinence with the picture I am trying to let you see.

Now, what does Jung identify as the eight personalities of humans?

1) The Extraverted Thinking Type

The Extraverted Thinking Type is a team of pure fact dealers. They are people who believe in facts and figures. They would rather judge based on available facts than how they feel about something. They are strictly logical and objective. They are fact-based, and sometimes, they might be cold to people. They are fair, highly organized, and strict to the core. A person like this is always impartial at work. They are straightforward and will not allow their prejudices to cloud their judgment in the evaluation of their staff. Julius Caesar, Jack Welsh, Napoleon Bonaparte, and several others belong to this category.

2) The Introverted Thinking Type

Introvert Thinking Types are the direct opposite of the Extraverted Thinking Types. What makes this class of people different is their attempt to picture big ideas. They try to comprehend complex ideas and try to figure out the ins and outs of a given situation. They will likely judge more by what appeals to them than what the facts seem to point out. Crises all happen in their heads. They often desire to learn more than the overview and internalize their experiences. Introverted Thinkers unconventionally solve problems. They are excellent at terminologies, and they dislike anyone who holds little regard for vocabularies and language standards. Charles Darwin, Bruce Lee, and Albert Einstein are handy examples of this class.

3) **The Extraverted Feeling Type**

A person with an extraverted feeling is a person who appeals to communal rather than personal tastes. In essence, their judgment, attitudes, opinions, and reactions are shaped by the values held in high esteem by the community. Rather than judge by the facts available or personal feelings, extraverted people incline towards what is considered right and wrong. An extraverted person has the tendency to be torn between facts and feelings. They are ethical, they hold high moral standards, and they may sometimes struggle to show what they sincerely believe in during certain situations.

4) **The Introverted Feeling Type**

The Introvert Feeling type isn't easy to spot in people. It is a style of life where people make decisions based on what they feel about people. It involves making decisions based on what you firmly hold as personal values, rather than facts and data. On the positive side, you may not notice the Introverted Feeling since it supports the natural laws of positive relations. If you are an Introverted Feeling type, you may choose never to tell a lie and maintain it as your value. When you decide to remain honest at critical times, it is almost hard, if not impossible, to know that you were realistic about a situation because it is your personal value.

If you were greedy, dishonest, or negative in any other perspective, however, it would become glaringly obvious that you made this decision for purely personal reasons. Warren Buffet, Jeff Bezos, Jimmy Carter, Tiger Woods, Mother Teresa, and several eminent personalities belong here.

5) The Extraverted Sensation Type

Excitement is the most distinguishing of people who have this personality. They are alive, "in the moment," and are overjoyed by their current experiences. They do not want to think about the past or future, and they hate being mellowed by people who do not share their enthusiasm. So, they'd rather hang out with people who belong to their sect. They are not interested in oppressing anyone, but they are tilted towards discrimination, thereby spurring an inferiority complex. Angelina Jolie, Bill Clinton, Lady Gaga, and Taylor Swift are people who reflect this personality.

6) The Introverted Sensation Type

This sect is the direct contrast of the extraverted class. Without even noticing, they do not appreciate much of the present moment. They dwell a lot more on the future and the past. They often find themselves wandering in their minds. They enjoy moments that are gone, and they long to be part of the past again.

If you belong to this category, it is no surprise that sometimes you linger on the past and wish you could bring it to life again. Often, you think about the future and try to imagine your chances of fixing your current problems in the future.

7) The Extraverted Intuitive Type

The spectacular feature of these people is their ability to brainstorm. They could be so fast and impressive that everyone else around them would not be able to keep up with the pace at which they think and solve problems. They can easily connect dots and patterns, and are articulate, vocal, and full of ideas. If this is you, you will be upset about how some people do not even seem to match half of your pace. You will be uneasy with their speed, and you will see what people are not telling you. Benjamin Franklin and Steve Wozniak belong to this category.

8) The Introverted Intuitive Type

The Introverted Intuitive belongs to a person who tries to be strategic in most cases. He is a big fan of theories and sophisticated systems, and he is good at recognizing patterns or trends. He can pick up hints from the past and connect the points to the future. The first problem is their inability to focus. They make brilliant investigators because they understand how to dig into the root cause problems. They do not necessarily become the boss; they are only strong enough to give futuristic insights to the boss. Hence, leaders should ensure they have such personalities around.

All said and done, it is essential to figure out who you are on the inside. You need to know who you are beyond the cultural claims, your uncertain psychology, and everything you have been told about yourself. You equally need to understand where you belong and how you fit in. Discovering who you are and who the people around you are can help you relate with them. It will help you to find YOUR PLACE and will also enable you to avoid being manipulated, which is crucial for survival!

Tips to remember

1. There are different personalities.
2. You need to figure out who you are outside the name, the culture, and everything life has thrown at you.
3. Try to think about other personalities.

CHAPTER 12
DETACHING FROM YOUR PARENTS AND WHATEVER HOLDS YOU BACK

Your parents are amongst the most active people in your life. They are top amongst the people who can influence your life, growth, development, and life policies. These people gave you your name, ethics, personality, and more than half of the living standards you have accepted and applied as your own. Parents hold so much influence that some of them become domineering and hold stakes in your life till adulthood. They understand you completely, and they can hack into your spirit in a way that you simply can't help telling them about your experience and applying their recommendations.

If you grew up in such families, leaving home would leave you with a double-sided feeling — you are excited, but also wondering how you will live the rest of your life. You will be delighted to get out of their wrenches, their autocratic tendencies, and their nauseating interference in your life. However, this should not be the case.

You have to leave your family at some point, but it certainly shouldn't be because they had a say in all of your life. Your parents should not be an obstacle to chasing your dreams. You should be able to pursue your desired goals without interference or opposition from your parents. This is why you must learn how to detach from your family. You need to be independent in your thinking, decisions, and aspirations. If you are still unsure how you can achieve that, the following tips will assist you in no small measures.

Tips to gain autonomy and mental independence

a. Get off their call

Are you always a call away from your parents? It is most likely the number one reason that your parents have a firm grip on you. The fact that you are always available the instant they call you points to the type of relationship you have with them. You believe that they deserve some love and respect, and you are trying to afford them this respect. This is just in line with Billy Graham's philosophy that "a child who is allowed to be disrespectful to his parents will not have true respect for anyone." By the way, these people didn't leave you when you were wrong. It would be absurd to leave them when they are growing old and weak.

Still, you have to create a space for personal growth and independence. Without sounding rude or disrespectful, you need to make it clear that you are an entirely different human. Much beyond being their offspring who would be at their beck and call, you are someone who needs to find your voice and independence, and you will not always be available. If you need to enroll in swimming, surfing, or boxing lessons, do whatever you can to keep off their unlimited calls and create times that you will be earnestly unavailable.

b. Put boundaries into effect

Setting boundaries is another effective way to wriggle out of manipulation from parents. As you grow into your 20s, you are becoming fully responsible for your life, and you need to express that when it matters. You will surely need suggestions from your parents, but you must draw a line over their interference. Make it doubly clear that there is a limit to their roles in your life. Your finances, relationship, career, and other aspects should not be in the hands of your parents, though they can guide you from their past experiences.

c. **Don't try to change them**

One other way to maintain mental independence from your parents is to make no effort to change them. Do not try to pressure them into changing; neither should you decide to make them change their lifestyle for you. Understand that your parents have chosen a distinct lifestyle that has become a part of them. They have cultivated and practiced these habits for most of their lives. You cannot expect them to thrash these behaviors simply because they do not go down well with you. Just so you know, trying to change your parents implies that you want them to change you too. As long as they accept giving up some things for you, you have to give up some of your liberty for them also. It reminds me of an old neighbor who wouldn't stop smoking until his military grandson made him do it — in turn, the young soldier had to quit his job.

d. Be mindful of what you share with them

Often, parents interfere in your affairs because you tabled these before them. They are your parents, and they want the best for you. They can understand a great deal about you; there is nothing awkward in all of these.

Nevertheless, it is crucial to draw a clear line with your parents. As a growing adult, you must learn to handle your problems on your own. You must learn to do without the recommendations or perspectives of anyone as you toil through your days. In particular, limit what you tell your parents if you do not want their imposing ideas floating around in your head and reflecting on your decisions.

e. Always have an exit strategy

An exit strategy is a fast way out of your family's imposition. It is any means by which you can avoid or escape their pressing demands. Your exit strategy must be handy and tailored to a particular situation. If your parents want you to be at their workplace, for instance, get yourself into something else that they can't refuse. Find activities that would make you so fixed that they are unwilling to raise their objections. Sometimes, you might have to visit a friend for weeks, travel elsewhere, or do anything that suffices as your exit strategy.

f. Don't try to reason with them

One of the easiest ways to weaken your resolution is to try to reason with your parents. When you reason with your parents, you try to consider the facts and figures in their recommendations. You are trying to figure how right or wrong they might be about your aspirations. A constant reality is that your parents are far more experienced than you. They can easily predict what might happen if events followed a particular pattern. You might be brilliant enough to see things in a different light and take different steps, but their fears that arouse from their experience can throw you off balance if you dare to let it sit in your mind. So, what is the best way out? Do not bother to reason with them. You will lose.

g. You don't have to spend the holidays with your parents

If you have left the family, you should begin to understand that you are gone for good. The earlier you see yourself belonging to a different family, the better. Your parents need to see you now and then, but you do not have to be back in their house. Whether you went to college or relocated for professional reasons, as long as you have chosen to live elsewhere, there is no reason you should holiday with your family anymore. You are no longer a part of them, and there is no mistaking that. Sitting with them again prompts you to tell them things you did not mean to, which infers that you would need their suggestions still.

All said and done, your independence is a requirement for self-discovery and self-reliance. If you cannot discover and depend solely on yourself, you will remain prey to the manipulation, oppression, and exploitation of the people who fill your world. Breaking off from your parents is one of the most difficult mental battles you need to fight without breaking the relationship with your family. Go through my suggestions again. You can make it work!

Tips to remember

1. If you want absolute independence, you need to be free from everyone, including your parents.

2. You have to detach from your parents, by all healthy means.

CHAPTER 13
THIS WILL MAKE YOU MENTALLY STRONG — TRY TO BELIEVE

According to the American Psychological Association, mental resilience is the *"process of adapting well in the face of adversity, trauma, threats, or even significant sources of stress."* This is exactly what you need as an individual making efforts to fight off manipulation. As you stand up to put a stop to constant oppression from friends, family, and several people who are dear to you, you need a lot of confidence. You need to bolster your spirit in a way that you can stand firm on your feet, no matter what goes wrong. It would be difficult to stand up to certain people, particularly those who hold a vital position in your life. Yet, you must remain calm and collected after standing up to oppression; you must be mentally resilient.

Brilliant psychologists, Clough and Strycharczyk, believe that mental resilience is essential for several reasons. There are also techniques for achieving mental resilience. They include the following:

1. Anxiety control

I spent the bulk of this book emphasizing anxiety and its effects. I tried to make you understand how crucial it is to keep your anxiety in control and never give yourself away to domineering hecklers. These rules must be painstakingly applied when you aspire to be mentally independent. I know it is absurd and unbelievable, but I want you to understand that staying on top of your anxiety is the number one way to be mentally healthy. It is one way you can keep yourself together without tearing yourself apart. If you are still unsure of how to keep yourself from getting too anxious, you should try reading the SELF section again, there is a lot to help you change!

2. Visualization and standards

Your standards are life ethics that you have decided to uphold. They are policies that you desire to live by and apply come hell or high water. Setting such standards can influence what you tolerate from people. It can also determine when you tell people that you are no longer willing to put up with their attitudes anymore. These standards can take away some of your so-called friends.

Nevertheless, knowing that you are on your life standards can be a cure to your soul. It can reassure you that you are not wrong even when everyone you cared about seems cross with you, and seeing your standards work hand in hand with your relationship with people is wonderful. So, set your living standards, visualize them, and stand by it!

3. Goal setting

Goal setting refers to your ability to set clear and concise goals. It implies that you can find "why" you do anything and what you stand to gain from it in the long run. Goal setting can help you underline who to stand up to, when you need to stand up, and why you have to stand up at all. The truth is that you cannot fight off every form of oppression in your life — some are not even at all overt. You should only fight those that get in the way of your dreams, and you can only identify them when you have got goals or dreams to start with. This implies that having thoughts is nonnegotiable. Set your goals and chase them!

4. Undying positivity

Positivity is the undying spirit to stay healthy and positive in the face of dying opposition. It is the fierce will to keep fighting hard and try even when all odds are clearly against you. Being positive implies that you are relentlessly optimistic. You can see the problems that would arise if you decided to cut some people off or give it back to their faces. Yet, you choose to stay healthy with the firm belief that you can make the best of whatever happens. Positivity is a burning fire in your heart that remains lit. It makes you remember that even when everyone is leaving you, there is some strong light down the end of the tunnel. Optimism is just what you need when you set out on a mission like this!

5. Patience, tenacity, and endurance

Who gets liberation without a lot of tenacity and endurance? You need to read about George Washington, Nelson Mandela, and John F. Kennedy to get solid ideas of how much it might cost a human to stand for what they believe in. You will likely not pay as much as they did, but the essence of the reference is to tell you how much you need tenacity. Even when things are going south with your best friends, parents, or even soulmate, you need to stay strong! Do not go back on your words, particularly if your actions are what you consider the best for your dreams and the standard you hope to build for yourself.

6. Self-validation

In the words of Amy Wayne, *"There is no greater source of inspiration and strength than the voices from inside you."* If these voices do not inspire, the external voices can do only a little to trigger your growth and inspire you. This is why you must make all efforts to motivate yourself before the world does at all. Use a lot of mantras; communicate with your inner self and make it clear that there are no mistakes about the path of life that you have chosen. Inspiration is motivation. Inspire yourself!

7. Be result-crazy

You need unmovable determination. You need to set your eyes on goals that are so clear that you can see them as you stare ahead, despite how far away they appear. Goals like these can drive you to move mountains and do things you have always feared you could not. That would include staying strong in the face of adversity. Your focus on your goals can help you to face any challenge, dare anyone who stands in the way of your dreams, and maintain your ground.

8. Tolerate discomfort

To wrap things up, I have to tell you that you need to tolerate a lot of discomforts. As I have proven in the earlier chapters, there are varying personalities. If you belong to a personality type that does not tolerate pain, you have to work yourself out to get this skill. The instant you begin to say "no" to people, they will be uncomfortable in several ways, and they will likely express it in their relations with you. Your parents may lock you out. Your boss might fire you, and your soulmate might call it quits. Some may not go to the extreme, but they will make sure it rubs off on you that they are not happy with you. Whatever discomfort you have to face, just brace for it. Fierce winds are coming!

Tips to remember

1. As you stand up to put a stop to constant oppression from friends, family, and several people who are dear to you, you need a lot of mental resilience and tenacity.

2. There are more than seven ways to be mentally strong, I listed them all here. Find your fit!

CHAPTER 14
3 NON-VERBAL WHITE PSYCHOLOGY TRICKS

From the start on to this moment in this book, we have extensively considered various methods to liberate yourself from Dark Psychology. We have spelled out several ways through which you can identify psychic hecklers and forever protect yourself from them. There are a series of related facts that you should understand, and I have put them forward in this book. I am going to wrap it up by picking out some facts in this chapter.

These facts have been underlined in some parts of the previous chapter. Nevertheless, it is vital to bring them all out. If they are all that you take out of this guide, they are enough to trigger a difference in you for the rest of your life. You should, of course, keep the lessons passed in every chapter in mind. These points are non-verbal media through which you can communicate your White Psychology to the world. What are they?

1. Read and give body language

More often than not, it is possible to tell that someone intends to manipulate you from their body language. If you pay close attention, you will realize that the twitch on their lips, the rise and fall of their eyebrows, and their gesticulation in general gives them away. If you pay just enough attention, you can tell a person who is looking to take advantage of you and stuff their ideas in your head. You can equally tell a person who has no malignant objectives.

Based on your observation, you can send strong signals back to potential exploiters with your body language. If you had been laughing all along and you realize your heckler has started the joke to pull a fast one on you, you should change. You might frown, get curious, or do anything to change your appearance. It has to be glaring that you are not falling for the trick. You need it!

2. Use mental math to avoid brainwashing

Mental math is my definition of fast-thinking that you do to find answers in a particular moment. It is an insightful calculation that you use to figure out the complication. It applies when you are in a mess and are finding your way out. You need it when you urgently need to think, evaluate, and decide how true or false a situation could be.

Your mental math is one of the most effective ways to slip off Dark psychologists and their tricks. Now and then, you should try to evaluate what you hear from people. Try to figure out whether what you heard was true, untrue, or entirely off point. It helps you to determine when someone was honest, tricky, reckless, or earnestly need to be changed.

3. Live the life you want

If you desire to live a lifestyle, you need to go all out and act it. You do not owe an apology or explanation to anyone for the life you have chosen. You deserve what you want, and you may never feel accomplished if you do not go for it. You can prove to psychic hecklers that they have nothing on you, and they can no longer hold you down by doing just what they didn't want you to do. You do not even have to say anything; just act. The maxim insists that actions speak a lot louder than words.

To cut a long story short, you are a unique person that should not be manipulated by anyone. You have to take every caution and precaution towards ensuring that it does not happen. If it is happening, it has to end, and if it has happened at some point in the past, it has got to come to an end. You will not practice Dark Psychology or make efforts to manipulate anyone. What the world needs is White Psychology!

TAKEAWAY

In the final analysis, it is important that you figure out what you truly long to do for the rest of your life. You need to note how you spend your energy and why you are spending it in this manner. Equally, you have to act out what you dream. I have developed White Psychology as a revolutionary psychology. My dream is to ensure that every human on Earth has the freedom to chase their dreams without oppression, influence, or manipulation from anyone.

If the world continues to believe in exploitation and manipulation, we will be worse off than what we are at the moment. Young men and women will rise and sleep with huge dreams; they will toil the streets every day with high hopes. But their dreams will always be crushed because they had to give up their beliefs, and their aspirations for someone else, as their minds were manipulated by their bosses, parents, colleagues, and people who were close to them.

But enough of these. Read this book from start to the end; you will come across White Psychology and you will never suffer the same old fate. I can guarantee that. If you have read it and picked some hints already, I have to say a big congratulations. You have learned why you must stand on your own and how to do it. You have learned the different personalities of people and how they can behave according to their nature.

As you learn the arts of White Psychology and venture into the world to apply them, you will need a lot of support and encouragement. You might also get into anxious moments that you cannot handle on your own. To help you through this moment, I have written a complementary 5k words long blog post about ANXIETY. And I will also be right there to support you as you find your voice.

You can reach me on my website www.frederiiick.com and sign up to my exclusive email list to benefit from the bonus content! And, of course, for more suggestions.

Last but not least: I would love to hear from you. Which principles have had the biggest impact? What successes have you seen? What advice would you give to others who are looking to overcome negative feelings and make everyday relationships extraordinary? Find me on Instagram at @frederickdonatone and let me know.

Finally, if these principles have made a positive impact in your life, please consider leaving a review on Amazon.com and/or passing a copy of the book along to a friend or family member. By leaving a review you'll get the eBook version of my next release – completely FREE! Reply to an email from me to claim your gift. See you next month with a new release!

ABOUT THE AUTHOR

Frederick III is a young man who created his own philosophy of well-being. His three fundamental principles are the Self, the Other and the Place; the balance of which leads to completeness. He promotes an overall and systemic vision of human beings and their relationships: the inner ones, between the plurality of the "Self " and the social ones.

"Society reflects what are the inner problems, like a mirror. The disintegrated, split personalities project their pathologies into the world squandering their energies."

"In a world that goes upside down, that is, that puts humans, their health, their rights, in the last place, it is necessary to recover the strength to react. We need to acquire tools and skills to be able to orient ourselves; we need to set out on the road."

Frederick has spent the last 5 years investigating the spectrum of the human mind, graduating in philosophy, living in every part of the world, and learning 5 languages. After 5 years, he is ready to put together the most active personalities in the world of change.